MIKE LEIGH

Two Thousand Years

ff

faber and faber

First published in 2006
by Faber and Faber Limited
3 Queen Square London WC1N 3AU

Typeset by Country Setting, Kingsdown, Kent CT14 8ES
Printed in England by Mackays of Chatham plc, Chatham, Kent

A CIP record for this book
is available from the British Library

ISBN 978-0-571-23236-9
ISBN 0-571-23236-1

2 4 6 8 10 9 7 5 3 1

Two Thousand Years

Mike Leigh's plays include: *Bleak Moments* (Open
Wholesome Glory (Royal Court Theatre Upstairs),
Silent Majority (Bush), *Babies Grow Old* (RSC),
Party, *Ecstasy*, *Goose-Pimples* and *Smelling a Rat*
(Hampstead), *Greek Tragedy* (Belvoir Street, Sydn
Edinburgh Festival and Stratford East), *It's a Grea*
Shame! (Stratford East). TV films: *Hard Labour*,
in May, *The Kiss of Death*, *Who's Who*, *Grown-Up*
Home Sweet Home, *Meantime*, *Four Days in July*
A Sense of History. TV studio plays: *The Permissi*
Society, *Knock for Knock*, *Abigail's Party*. Radio pl
Too Much of a Good Thing. Feature films: *Bleak Mom*
The Short and Curlies, *High Hopes*, *Life is Sweet*, *Na*
Secrets and Lies, *Career Girls*, *Topsy-Turvy*, *All or*
Nothing, *Vera Drake*.

also by Mike Leigh

screenplays

NAKED AND OTHER SCREENPLAYS
SECRETS AND LIES
CAREER GIRLS
TOPSY-TURVY
ALL OR NOTHING

plays

ABIGAIL'S PARTY and GOOSE-PIMPLES
(Penguin)
ECSTASY with SMELLING A RAT
(Nick Hern Books)

Introduction

Here's my Jewish play. I've been threatening to do it for years, but I haven't felt ready until now, when I'm well into my sixties.

All my films and plays have in one way or another dealt with identity. Who are you? What are you? Who is the real you, and who the persona defined by other people's expectations or preconceptions? *Secrets and Lies* was about a woman seeking the truth about her identity; *Vera Drake* told the story of the heroine's hidden life; *Abigail's Party* explored received notions of social behaviour; *Topsy-Turvy* was about reality and artifice; and *Naked* and *High Hopes* were each concerned, in quite different ways, with the conflict between what we are and how we live, with what we believe in.

'You're born Jewish. You are as you are,' says Dave in *Two Thousand Years*. And Tammy says, 'It's not the whole of me – I feel Jewish, and I don't feel Jewish.' Those of us who escaped from our Jewish background have usually spent most of our adult lives keeping quiet about our Jewishness, at least in public. This isn't about being ashamed of one's identity, it's rather about not wanting to be perceived as being something you're actually not, or being cast in a stereotype role that isn't your true self.

I grew up in Salford, that great industrial city that sits side by side with Manchester, by what in those days was the filthy River Irwell. And, although I've lived in London since I was seventeen, I still feel very much a northerner. Lancashire is in my blood, my humour, my accent, and in my down-to-earth, no-nonsense attitudes. It's part of my identity – as Tammy says, of being Jewish, it's 'just part of who I am'.

But I also feel very Jewish. In fact, Manchester Jewish – a very specific condition, with its own abrasive sense of humour. There has been a big Jewish population in Manchester since the mid-nineteenth century, and the atmosphere in which I grew up was very typical of that world, except for two things.

My father was a local GP, and for the first thirteen years of my life we lived over the surgery in a totally working-class district of North Salford, where I attended the local state primary and grammar schools. So I grew up as a middle-class Jewish kid in a working-class, predominantly non-Jewish area. This endowed me with a certain duality of social identity, and a clear sense of cultural and class divisions, both of which have undoubtedly informed all my work.

The other exception was that our extended family were Zionists, which not all Jews were in the 1940s and 1950s, although there had always been something of a Zionist tradition in Manchester. My paternal great-grandfather edited a Zionist newspaper in Blackburn long before the First World War, my maternal aunts both emigrated, one to Palestine, the other after it became Israel, and my parents met each other in the Zionist youth movement referred to in the play, and to which I belonged as a teenager.

Tammy reflects on how, for some people, the word Zionism has changed from meaning 'something positive and hopeful' to being 'a dirty word'. Certainly, the confusion and frustration about Israel and Palestine shared by many liberal Jews comes out of once having believed passionately in an enlightened, secular, socialist

Jewish State. And *Two Thousand Years* is an expression of these feelings.

Of course, the play is set in London, not in Manchester, but then it isn't directly autobiographical. However, as a non-believer, I have always been inspired by stories of my paternal great-grandmother, Rachel Blain, who died just a few weeks before I was born in 1943, and whose first great-grandchild I would have been. Legend has it that she loathed and detested rabbis, and she was known to chuck them out of her house with her bare hands. The healthy influence of this formidable lady could be felt throughout our family during my childhood, and I owe something of this play to her.

Of course, what nobody could have foreseen in the 1950s was the extent to which religious fanaticism would come to afflict the world as it has. The confusion of a young person who turns to religion is a phenomenon of our strange times, although *Two Thousand Years* doesn't pretend to explain away Josh's dilemma in easy, simplistic terms.

In fact, like all my work, this play is reflective rather than didactic. My job is always to raise questions, and to leave you to ponder, to debate, to argue and, indeed, to reflect about things, rather than to walk away and forget the whole experience.

Two Thousand Years is about caring and togetherness, generosity and selfishness, love and anger, hope and disappointment, and life and death. In other words, it's about families and politics. It is both a Jewish play, and a play for and about everybody.

Mike Leigh
London, January 2006

Two Thousand Years was first performed in the Cottlesloe auditorium of the National Theatre, London, on 15 September 2005. The cast was as follows:

Rachel Caroline Gruber
Danny Allan Corduner
Josh Ben Caplan
Jonathan Adam Godley
Tammy Alexis Zegerman
Dave John Burgess
Tzachi Nitzah Sharron
Michelle Samantha Spiro

Director Mike Leigh
Designer Alison Chitty
Lighting Designer Paul Pyant
Music Gary Yershon
Sound Designer John Leonard

Characters

Rachel
Danny
Josh
Jonathan
Tammy
Dave
Tzachi
Michelle

TWO THOUSAND YEARS

Setting

*The action takes place in the living room
of Rachel and Danny's house in Cricklewood,
North London. A Victorian semi.*

*The two ground-floor rooms have been merged,
by the removal of a dividing wall. The atmosphere
is bright and informal. White walls; stripped
and varnished floorboards and woodwork;
bright rugs; comfortable contemporary furniture.
A full bookshelf unit, with all kinds of modern books.
In what was the front room sit a big sofa and
an armchair. Back to back with the armchair
is a smaller sofa, facing into the old rear room,
which contains a table and chairs, a television,
and double doors into a conservatory. This is full
of plants, and opens into a garden with trees.
Popular prints on the wall (Picasso, Matisse).
Side tables, newspapers, magazines. A sideboard
with assorted things, including a few bottles –
whisky, gin, etc. The door to the old front room
is kept permanently closed, with a large plant
in front of it. Through the other, operational door,
the staircase is visible.*

Act One

Lights up. July, 2004. A Saturday. Late afternoon. Bright, sunny. The conservatory doors are open.
    Rachel sits in the armchair, reading a book. Danny sits back to back with her, on the small sofa, reading the Guardian. *Josh is sprawled on the big sofa. He is surrounded by several books, one of which he is reading. A mug stands near him on the floor.*

Pause.

Rachel Have you finished that article?

Danny Not quite.

Rachel What do you think?

Danny I'm confused. One minute I agree with him, the next minute I don't.

Rachel I know what you mean.

    Pause.
    The front doorbell rings. Danny and Rachel look at each other. Josh doesn't notice. Danny gets up, glances at Josh, and goes out to answer the front door. The following can be heard:

Jonathan (*off*) Hi, Danny.

Danny (*off*) Jonathan!

Jonathan (*off*) I was just passing – is it convenient?

Danny (*off*) Of course. Come in.

Jonathan (*off*) How are you?

Danny (*off*) I'm well, thanks. How are you?

Jonathan (*off*) Very good.

Danny (*off*) Great. Go in, go in.

Jonathan (*entering*) Is everybody home?

Danny (*following*) Not quite.

Jonathan has entered the room. He is holding an open box containing some salad vegetables. Rachel gets up and goes to greet him.

Jonathan Hello, Rachel.

Rachel Hello, Jonathan.

They kiss cheeks.

Danny It's the market gardener, come bearing gifts.

Rachel We haven't seen you in ages.

Jonathan Listen, we've all been busy. I come with a burnt offering.

Rachel What have you got for us?

Jonathan A cucumber, some courgettes; and look at that lettuce.

Rachel It looks fabulous.

Jonathan They came up really well this year.

Danny It's all the rain we've been having.

Jonathan You're right. So . . . enjoy.

He hands Rachel the box.

Rachel Thank you. D'you want a cup of tea?

Jonathan I'd love one. I can't stop long. I'll keep the box.

Rachel Okay.

She goes out with the box. Josh gets up.

Jonathan Josh! How's it going, mate?

Josh Alright, thanks. And yourself?

Jonathan Yeah – good, thanks.

Josh drifts into the other half of the room.

Danny Sit, sit!

Jonathan sits down.

Jonathan So how're things?

Danny Can't complain. Busy. And you?

Jonathan Hectic.

Danny How's the new job?

Jonathan Well, you know . . . One housing department's pretty much like another.

Danny But you're happy?

Jonathan Yeah.

Danny Good. Where d'you get your boots?

Jonathan Er . . . I can't remember. I've had 'em for years.

Danny Yeah? Comfortable?

Jonathan Yeah. This one lets in a bit of water . . . but, yeah – they're good.

Danny Have you seen this article in today's paper?

Jonathan Yeah, I have. I read it this morning.

Danny I don't know about you, but it made me very uncomfortable.

He sits down. Rachel enters with a cup of tea for Jonathan.

5

Jonathan It makes *me* very uncomfortable. But let's face it, anything that questions the crap we were fed about Camp David's a bonus . . .

Danny Yeah, I suppose so.

Jonathan Barak offers everything; Arafat accepts nothing; Barak's the good guy, Arafat's the bad guy . . .

Danny The Israelis have totally emasculated Arafat. He sits there, all alone in one room in his compound in Ramallah, surrounded by Israeli troops . . .

Jonathan He can't do a thing.

Danny He's got no control.

Rachel (*sitting*) He's such a saint, Arafat?

Jonathan Granted he's not a saint. But you don't chop a man's arms off, and then complain he doesn't shake your hand.

Rachel No, of course not; but there's intransigence and stupidity on both sides, isn't there?

Danny Well, no one said there isn't.

Rachel I know no one said there isn't!

Jonathan Yeah, but the two sides are not evenly matched.

Rachel That's also true. I just think this goes too far. (*indicating newspaper*) I mean, who's he benefiting by whitewashing Arafat? Have a biscuit, Jonathan.

Jonathan Thanks. (*He takes one.*)

Danny Have you read this article, Josh?

Josh is now sitting at the table.

Josh No, not yet.

Danny He says that Israel instigated the Intifada. Do you believe that?

Jonathan I believe it – why not?

Rachel It was politically expedient for them.

Danny Yeah – well, of course.

Jonathan He talks about the fascists in Israeli military intelligence who are directing government policy.

Rachel I find that very alarming.

Jonathan It is alarming.

Danny It's terrifying. He also says that, based on false Israeli intelligence, the US invaded Iraq.

Jonathan And are you so sure that wasn't the case?

Danny Well, how can we know?

Rachel Yes, but even if the Israelis did pass on false intelligence to the Americans, they would never have invaded Iraq unless it suited them. The Americans do what Americans want to do.

Jonathan You believe Sharon'll quit Gaza next year?

Danny No. Of course not.

Rachel It's hard to imagine.

Danny I reckon it's just a bluff. There you go, Josh.

He gets up, and gives Josh the newspaper.

Josh Thanks.

Danny So, Jonathan: have you been suffering with greenfly this year?

Jonathan Oh, terrible!

Rachel It's a nightmare.

Jonathan Everybody, all the allotments. A good tip: couple of drops of washing-up liquid in a water squirter, they hate it. Greenfly, blackfly – you blitz the lot.

Danny Really?

Jonathan Yeah.

Danny I didn't know that. It doesn't harm the plants?

Jonathan No, just a couple of drops.

Danny Hm!

Rachel How's Sally?

Jonathan She's great. She sends her love – she's gone to see her folks.

Rachel How is she?

Jonathan Well, she's . . . y'know; working too hard, but she's fine.

Rachel Send her our love.

Jonathan I will do. (*Pause.*) And how's Tammy?

Rachel Oh, she's wonderful.

Danny (*simultaneously*) Terrific.

Rachel She's so busy, we hardly ever see her.

Danny She's flying all over the place.

Rachel She was in Brussels a couple of months ago.

Danny Doing some work for Amnesty International.

Jonathan Fantastic!

Rachel At a conference on Guantanemo Bay. Translating for a Spanish newspaper.

Jonathan You must be very proud.

Danny Listen . . .

Rachel Yes, we are proud.

Josh goes and stands by the conservatory door.

Danny Yeah, we are proud. She's about to go back to Venezuela.

Jonathan Really?

Rachel She feels it's important.

Danny She's only going on holiday this time.

Jonathan That was a terrible experience for her.

Rachel She's very strong.

Jonathan Are you going away this year?

Danny Yeah –

Rachel Yeah, we're going to Gozo.

Jonathan That's in North Africa?

Rachel It's a little island off Malta.

Danny (*simultaneously*) . . . Malta.

Jonathan Oh, yeah.

Danny What about you?

Jonathan Rome.

Danny Really?

Rachel Oh, we were there in the spring.

Jonathan Yeah?

Rachel For a long weekend, weren't we?

Danny We were.

Jonathan See you, Josh!

Josh has come back into the room, and has left, closing the door behind him.

Rachel It was my consolation prize for turning fifty.

Jonathan I can't believe you're fifty.

Rachel You were a bit slow on the uptake there, Jonathan. I can't believe I'm fifty, either.

Danny But you are.

Rachel Yeah, I know I am – thank you!

Danny We had a wonderful time, though, didn't we?

Rachel Yes, we did.

Danny Have you been before?

Jonathan No.

Rachel You'll love it.

Danny We weren't too sure about the Vatican, though, were we?

Rachel That's true.

Danny No, all that wealth, and then you go outside . . .

Rachel . . . and there's thirty or forty beggars on the steps of St Peter's. There's all the gold inside, and then you come outside . . .

Jonathan . . . and there's all the poverty.

Rachel Exactly.

Danny It's the hypocrisy.

Pause.

Jonathan I still can't believe you're fifty.

Rachel Thank you.

Danny So how old are you now, Jonathan?

Jonathan Forty.

Danny No!

Jonathan Yeah; Sally'll be forty in December.

Danny How did that happen?

Jonathan I don't know – I don't feel it.

Danny Well, I don't feel fifty-three.

Rachel Of course he's forty.

Danny What d'you mean?

Rachel Well, my sister's going to turn forty next year, isn't she? She was born in 1965. You're forty!

Jonathan Have you heard from Mash recently?

Danny Not a word.

Rachel She sent us a change-of-address card – when was that?

Danny Two, three years ago?

Jonathan Yeah?

Rachel Out of the blue, we suddenly get this printed card – no note: 'Michelle Rosen is now at . . . Devonshire Mews, somewhere . . . '

Danny W1, very sprauncy.

Rachel No message. I didn't feel I could phone. So I sent her some very nice flowers, and a card.

Jonathan D'you hear anything back?

Danny No.

Rachel Nothing.

Jonathan When did you last see her?

Danny A long time.

Rachel Shortly after my fortieth birthday – ten years ago.

Danny Ten years.

Rachel (*simultaneously*) Ten years. My mum and dad haven't seen her. (*Pause.*) I try not to think about it.

Pause.

Jonathan I haven't seen her for twenty years.

Rachel Is it as long as that?

Jonathan Of course, she was at university – I went up to Leeds to see her. That's when we split up. We were just kids.

Pause.

Danny So how old were you when you first came to this house?

Jonathan Sixteen.

Danny No!

Jonathan Yeah.

Rachel I remember . . . she was so pleased with herself – wasn't she?

Danny She was. They came to baby-sit – you came to baby-sit, didn't you?

Jonathan Yep. It's funny, remembering. I can still see her up at Finchley Road, dancing, twice as fast as everybody else, like a Whirling Dervish.

Rachel Sounds like her.

Danny All that Israeli dancing – remember?

Rachel *Rikudim* – how could anyone forget?

Danny We used to keep going for hours – how did we do it?

Rachel We didn't stop – if you stopped, you got tired, so we carried on all night. We'd be dancing the *Hora* at two o'clock in the morning!

Jonathan And it didn't matter if you could dance, or you couldn't dance, or if you had a wooden leg . . .

Danny Yeah, well that's what it was all about, the spirit of the Movement – the *ruach* . . .

Jonathan (*simultaneously*) The *ruach* . . .

Danny (*continues*) . . . It didn't matter who we were, nobody judged you, everybody was equal . . .

Rachel That's right.

Danny And then, when you went to camp, you took out your pocket money, you pooled your resources, and you shared it out.

Rachel 'From each according to his ability, to each according to his needs.'

Jonathan And we loved it. And we believed it. And we lived it. And then, at sixteen, you went to Israel for six weeks, you went on *kibbutz*, and they're actually living it, and it all makes sense – the great socialist dream.

Rachel It was very seductive.

Jonathan Ach, at sixteen it was seductive.

Danny That's what they were preparing us for.

Jonathan The whole propaganda machine.

Danny Have you still got your blue shirt?

Jonathan No. You got yours?

Rachel No. I've still got Tammy's, though.

Danny Have you?

Rachel I just haven't got round to throwing it away.

Jonathan Well, I should be going.

Rachel Weren't you going to go on *Aliyah*?

Jonathan Yeah, I was going to go on *Aliyah*.

Rachel So what happened, you changed your mind?

Jonathan What happened? Israel happened. It changed. I got disillusioned. I decided I belonged here after all. Would you go there now?

Danny No.

Jonathan Would you want to live on a kibbutz?

Danny No way.

Rachel I was born on a kibbutz.

Jonathan Of course.

Rachel I spent the first four-and-a-half years of my life living in a children's home. My parents came back to this country because my mother found it so unacceptable that she couldn't live with her child. My father would have stayed there quite happily. Let me tell you something, Jonathan. As far as I'm concerned, the Great Kibbutz Ideology was all very well for the men, but for the women . . . Their children were taken away from them as soon as they were born, to free them up to do their bit for the Great Zionist Dream; and they ended up *shlepping* for the whole kibbutz. And when I went back there at the age of eighteen, nothing had changed. I spent six months, either in the laundry, or in the kitchens, washing up three times a day for four hundred people, until my hands were peeling so badly they sent me to chop the vegetables that the men had picked in the beautiful hills of Galilee. So, no, I wouldn't want to go and live in a kibbutz, thank you very much. I'll get your box for you, Jonathan.

She gets up and goes out.

Jonathan Well; there you go.

Jonathan and Danny get up and move towards the door.

Danny So, Hymie's crossing the road in Golders Green, and he's knocked over by a Number 13 bus. And he's lying there in the road, and he's in a bad way. And a crowd gathers round him. And a priest is walking by, and he hears this – (*Groans.*) – groaning, and so he goes over to have a look. And he kneels down beside Hymie, and starts giving him the last rites – you know, erm, 'Do you believe in God the Father, God the Son, and God the Holy Spirit?' And, erm, Hymie looks up, and he says, 'I'm lying here dying, and he asks me riddles!'

Pause. Rachel has entered with the empty box and some flowers. She stands by the door.

Rachel Don't feel you have to laugh, Jonathan.

Danny Well, I think it's funny.

Jonathan No, it's very good – I'll tell Sally.

Danny Yeah, well, she'll like it.

Rachel Oh – here's your box. And give her these.

Jonathan Oh, thank you very much. They're beautiful.

Rachel They're from the garden.

Jonathan Say hi to Tammy for me.

Rachel We will.

Jonathan Is Josh –?

Danny Oh he's doing his thing.

Jonathan It's lovely to see you both.

Rachel And you, Jonathan.

Danny sees Jonathan out.

Danny (*off*) Thanks for popping round.

Jonathan (*off*) It's a pleasure.

Danny (*off*) Take care.

Jonathan (*off*) See you soon.

Danny (*off*) I'll see you soon, yeah.

Jonathan (*off*) 'Bye.

Danny (*off*) All the best – 'bye.

The front door closes. Rachel has started clearing up the tea things. Danny returns.

Thanks very much!

Rachel It isn't that funny.

Danny Well, I think it is.

Rachel I'm only teasing you. Come on, give me a hand.

He does so.

Danny Nice guy, Jonathan.

Rachel Yeah, it's a shame for them, isn't it?

Danny D'you think they'll adopt?

Rachel No. She only just had a miscarriage a couple of months ago. I think they'll keep trying.

Danny Yeah. Maybe you're right.

Danny has followed Rachel out to the kitchen. Fade to blackout.

SCENE TWO

Lights up. August 2004. A weekday. Mid-morning. Rachel is dusting. The conservatory doors are closed. Enter Josh with a mug of tea and a book.

Rachel Good morning!

Josh Alright, Mum?

He glances around the room, looking for something.

Rachel They're over here.

Josh What?

Rachel Your glasses.

Josh Where?

She takes his spectacles from the bookshelf and gives them to him.

Cheers.

He sits in the armchair, and opens his book. He glances up. She has been watching him.

What?

Rachel Nothing. What d'you mean, 'What?'

Josh You were looking at me.

Rachel So I can't look at my own son, now?

She plumps the cushions. Pause.

Josh What're you doing today?

Rachel I'm here – I'm busy. Your dad and I are going away in a couple of days. I've got a lot to do. I've got to pack. What are you doing today, more to the point?

Rachel continues dusting and polishing. Josh sits back and sighs.

What's the matter now?

Josh I was just thinking.

Rachel Don't tire yourself out. What about?

Josh I think I'll go for a walk.

Rachel looks at Josh. She is not pleased. She turns round, and walks straight out. Josh sighs and rubs his eyes. Fade to blackout.

SCENE THREE

Lights up. August 2004. A weekday. Late morning. The conservatory doors are closed.
Josh is pacing around the room in a very anxious state. A carrier bag is on the sofa. After a while, he picks it up and puts it on the smaller sofa. He pauses and looks at it. Kids can be heard playing somewhere nearby. Josh goes to the conservatory doors and closes the curtains, and returns his attention to the carrier bag. Pause. He takes off his watch and places it on the arm of the sofa. He rolls up his left shirtsleeve. Then he takes several items out of the carrier bag and lays them out on the sofa. The first of these is a maroon Jewish skull-cap, which he puts on his head, fastening it to his hair with a clip. Next is part of a set of phylacteries (tefillin), which, after a moment's pause, he attaches to the upper part of his bare arm. Then he says a prayer in Hebrew, half-audibly:

Josh

Baruch Atah adonai eloheinu,
melech ha'olam. Asher kidishanu
bemitzvotav v'tsivanu l'haniach
tefillin.

In the distance, the sounds of an ambulance and a
police car. Josh now binds the black strap round his
arm, and fixes the other part of the set of phylacteries
to his head. He picks up a prayer book, opens it, pauses,
and puts it down. Then he tears the phylacteries from
his head and from his arm, takes off the skull-cap,
turns back to the conservatory, and opens one curtain
a little. He stares out at the garden. Pause. Blackout.

SCENE FOUR

Lights up. August 2004. A Sunday. Very early morning.
The room is dark. The hall light is on. Enter Rachel and
Danny, carrying holiday luggage, which they leave in the
room. They immediately go upstairs, taking off their
travelling anoraks as they go. Blackout.

SCENE FIVE

Lights up. Early morning. August 2004. A couple of
hours or so later. Josh is standing in profile in the
conservatory, the doors of which are open. He wears his
skull-cap, and is reading aloud, but very quietly, from his
prayer book. He is, in fact, praying. After a while, the
door opens, and Rachel enters from the hall. She is
wearing pyjamas. She is unaware of Josh. She picks up
her bag, which is on the sofa. She turns and sees Josh.
Shocked, she drops her bag to the floor. Josh looks up.
He stops praying.

19

Josh Hello, Mum.

Rachel What are you doing?

He comes into the room.

Josh I was praying.

Rachel What?!

Josh How was your holiday?

Rachel stares at him. She is speechless. Josh walks past her quickly, and goes upstairs. She watches him. Then she rushes to the conservatory doors, closes them, and rushes upstairs. Blackout.

SCENE SIX

Lights up. August 2004. Later on the same day. Bright sunlight. The conservatory doors are open. Josh is sitting on the sofa. He is wearing his skull-cap. Danny is pacing. He is wearing shorts. Enter Rachel. She sits in the armchair.

Josh Why don't you say anything?

Rachel What's to say? We don't know what to say.

Danny I don't understand, Josh. It's beyond me. It's unbelievable. It's like having a Muslim in the house.

Rachel Danny!

Danny Alright, then, a Martian!

Josh I'm still me – I haven't changed.

Danny Of course you've changed!

Josh I haven't!

Danny Well, what's that thing on your head?

Rachel We still love you, Josh.

Danny Of course we do.

Josh It's not a thing, it's a *capple*.

Rachel Look, Josh: we go away for two weeks; we come back, and – this . . .

Danny sits on the sofa.

Danny What I want to know is . . . what's it all about? What's been going on? Where's it come from?

Rachel Josh?

Josh It comes from me.

Rachel What d'you mean, it comes from you?

Danny So you read a few books, and suddenly you're a *frummer*?

Rachel How can it just come from you? Have you been influenced by people, some kind of sect. The *Chassidim*?

Danny Those *Luboviches*, or something? What, you're not going to tell us?

Josh You don't understand.

Rachel We're trying to understand.

Danny Have you been going to a synagogue?

Josh Sometimes.

Danny Really? For how long?

Pause.

Josh I've been going to see someone.

Rachel Who have you been going to see?

Josh (*shouting*) A rabbi – alright?!

Rachel So how come you know rabbis, all of a sudden?

Danny (*cod Yiddish accent*) Vot, a *rebbe* mit a long vite beard?

Josh It's not a joke!

Danny You're right! It's not a joke!

Josh It just makes sense.

Danny (*getting up*) Sense? It makes no sense.

Josh (*getting up*) Look, I don't want to talk about this now!

Danny Oh, you never want to talk about anything, Josh!

Josh (*shouting*) What's it got to do with you?!

Rachel We're your parents!

Danny has picked up a pile of unopened post.

Danny What's it got to do with us? I'll tell you what it's got to do with us. You live under our roof. We feed you, we clothe you, we don't complain. Your mother runs around clearing up after you, while I spend all day fiddling in people's mouths. We give you money, you buy books, you stay up half the night, you get up whenever you like, you're free to come and go. You've never had a job. Josh: you left university seven years ago with a First Class Honours degree in mathematics – the world was your oyster. We tried to bring you up decently and respectably, and now this *mishigas*! You're crazy, you're off your head! We've got a postcard from Tammy.

Josh I'm sorry I'm such a disappointment to you!

He goes out, slamming the door.

Rachel You did that on purpose!

Danny What?

Rachel You're always comparing them! Why the postcard from Tammy at that moment? You know what he's like!

Danny It was here in my hand. D'you want to read it?

Rachel No, I don't want to read it! I'll look at it later.

Danny Alright – fine!

Danny sits on the sofa. Pause.

Rachel Now what?

Danny God knows.

Rachel I mean, what's he going to eat? Will he want to go kosher?

Danny I don't know.

Rachel Well, he'd better not expect us to go kosher – I'm not having it.

Danny Nor am I. Over my dead body.

Pause.

Rachel That's why he hasn't touched the bacon.

Danny What, there's bacon?

Rachel There's an unopened packet of unsmoked organic in the fridge.

Danny Is it past its sell-by date?

Rachel No, of course it isn't. I bought it for him before we went away.

Danny Right, I'm starving. I'm going to have bacon and eggs.

He gets up and makes for the door. She follows him.

Rachel You're not serious. You're not going to make bacon and eggs today?!

Danny Today, tomorrow – what difference?

Rachel Danny, you're making a statement, like an adolescent!

Danny It's my house, and if I want bacon and eggs, I'll have bacon and eggs.

He goes out. She follows.

Rachel Well, I'm not having any.

Danny You don't have to.

Rachel Not today, anyway.

Blackout.

SCENE SEVEN

Lights up. August 2004. The following Sunday afternoon. A sunny day. The conservatory doors are open.
    Josh is standing in the room, looking out to the garden. He is holding a glass of water.
    Enter Rachel, Tammy and Danny.

Rachel (*coming in*) Leave the washing up. We'll do it later.

Tammy Thanks for lunch, Mum. Or do I mean breakfast? My brain's five hours behind the rest of my body.

She slumps down on the sofa.

Danny What time did you get in?

Tammy Eleven a.m. GMT, and six a.m. in Caracas – oh, and three p.m. in Beijing.

Danny D'you want a little *shluff*?

Tammy No, it's better to keep partying. Presents!

She gets up, and starts taking things out of a large carrier bag.

Right: Dad first – sorry I missed your birthday. (*She gives him an item.*) From El Hatillo, on the coast.

Danny What is it, a dress?

Tammy No, it's a shroud. Mum . . .

She gives Rachel a small packet.

Rachel What's this?

Tammy Half a kilo of cocaine. It's Venezuelan coffee, Mum.

Rachel Thank you!

Danny (*having unravelled it*) Oh Tammy, it's a hammock!

Tammy I thought you could hang it between the fruit trees.

She gives Josh a small item.

Josh . . .

Josh (*unenthusiastically*) Thanks.

Tammy (*in Spanish*) *Chocolate.*

Josh I know.

Tammy I'm sure you know.

Danny Thanks, darling – it's lovely!

Tammy Oh, it's a pleasure, Daddy! So . . . what about my prezzies from Gozo?

She sits on the sofa.

Rachel D'you know what? We left them on the plane.

Tammy *Madre mia!*

Rachel Don't swear at me!

Danny I've always wanted a hammock. Thank you!

Tammy So, Dad: about this shaggy jellyfish story . . .

Danny Yes?

Tammy So, what? Did you wrestle it to the bottom of the seabed, like Hercules?

Danny No, I ran out, as fast as I could.

Rachel He ran around the beach, screaming his head off. It was hilarious.

Danny I wasn't screaming. I was shouting.

Rachel The whole of Gozo could hear you.

Tammy I thought you said you were being brave.

Danny It was the bravest thing I've ever done.

Tammy laughs.

Don't laugh. Have you ever been stung by a jellyfish?

Tammy No, but I really should try it sometime.

Danny Well, it hurts.

Rachel *Och a nebbish!*

Josh is now sitting near the conservatory, reading a book.

Tammy You alright, Josh?

Josh Yeah, why?

Tammy Just checking on your welfare state.

Josh What's that supposed to mean?

Tammy Nothing.

Pause.

Rachel So, are you glad you went back to Venezuela?

Tammy Yeah . . . it was something that I just had to do – d'you know what I mean?

Rachel Yes. I do.

Danny So what's it like now, Caracas?

Tammy Oh, it's amazing, it's . . . like the floods never happened.

Rachel Really?

Tammy Yeah. Well, the last time I was there, Caracas was crackers, let's face it.

Rachel Don't remind me. We were worried sick, weren't we?

Danny We were.

Rachel So what was happening?

Tammy The referendum.

Danny What referendum?

Rachel We read about it in the *Guardian*.

Tammy Yeah, it was fascinating.

Danny Oh, yeah.

Tammy The Americans tried to get rid of Chavez.

Rachel The Americans were involved?

Tammy Yeah. Bush wants their oil, doesn't he?

Danny Ah, yes.

Rachel Of course he does.

Tammy Anyway, Chavez won. It was electric – thousands of people on the streets. We stayed up all night.

Danny Did you?

Tammy Yeah, it was brilliant.

Rachel Sounds it.

Tammy And d'you know what? There was a seventy per cent turnout.

Rachel Seventy per cent? Blimey.

Danny Well, if there's something to vote for, people turn out.

Rachel And they had something to vote for. Here, we've only got things to vote against. If there was a viable alternative to Tony Blair, we'd have a seventy per cent turnout here next year. But there isn't, so we won't. And he'll get his third term, the jammy bugger!

Tammy Hold on, people do turn out – look at the anti-war demos.

Danny Politicians don't give a shit about demonstrations any more.

Rachel They never did, Danny. They're just more cynical about it now.

Tammy No, you're more cynical.

Danny Yeah, maybe you're right. Maybe we've all lost hope.

Josh What d'you mean, Dad?

Danny Well, we used to have ideals, Josh. Politics used to be about ideals. But not any more.

Rachel Now it's just about single issues.

Tammy What's a single issue? There are no single issues. When we marched against the war, it wasn't about Iraq, it was about a whole load of other things as well.

Rachel There's plenty to march about.

Tammy Yeah, there is.

Josh People aren't happy.

Tammy Are you going to vote next year, Josh?

Josh I might vote Green.

Tammy Green? Not maroon?

Maroon is the colour of Josh's skull-cap.
Pause.

Nice hat, by the way.

Rachel Tammy!

Danny (*simultaneously*) Tammy!

Josh It's not a hat.

Tammy Sorry – *kippah*.

Josh It's a *capple*.

Tammy *Capple, kippah* – potayto, potahto . . . (*Pause.*)
You know, I haven't seen you wearing one of those since
your *bar mitzvah*.

Danny That's enough!

Rachel (*simultaneously*) Tammy!

Josh is pacing around.

Josh (*shouting*) If you've got something to say, Tammy,
just say it!

Danny Josh, *please*!

Josh You've sat through the whole of lunch with a smirk
on your face, and said nothing. Now you sit there on
your fat arse, taking the piss. If you've got something to
ask, then ask!

Tammy Alright, chill out! (*Pause.*) Actually, I do have something to ask you.

Josh What?

Tammy (*little girl voice*) Do you really think my arse is fat?

Josh Yeah, I do.

Tammy Thank you very much.

Josh Oh, forget it.

   Pause.

Tammy So, what, have you been learning Hebrew?

Josh What're you getting at?

Tammy I was just wondering if you're praying in Hebrew.

Josh (*shouting*) Of course I'm praying in Hebrew!

Tammy Alright – well done!

Josh Why d'you want to know?

Tammy I'm just interested.

Danny So Thursday morning, this little kid comes in, and he craps himself in the chair, he's so scared. His mother was mortified. Poor Estelle had to come in and help me clear up the mess. Nothing wrong with his teeth. Put me back ten minutes.

Rachel Put you back ten minutes – put him back for life! He'll probably never go to the dentist again, poor kid!

Tammy Did it bring back happy memories, Dad?

Danny What d'you mean?

Tammy Changing our nappies.

Rachel That was a long time ago, thank God.

Josh Now look at us.

Rachel Exactly.

Josh starts pacing round the room. Rachel has been looking at one of Josh's books.

Josh, it says on the back of this book you're reading that if the Jews were to stick to all the Laws of the *Torah*, they'd create a just and caring society that the rest of the world could emulate, and that's the reason that God gave the Land of Israel to the Jewish people. Well, I'm sorry, but I've got a problem with that, on two counts. First of all, is Israel a just and caring society? I shouldn't think the Palestinians think so. And, secondly, do you really believe that God gave Israel to the Jews?

Josh It's just what's written in the Bible, Mum.

Rachel Yeah, and – ?

Josh And some people believe it, and some don't.

Tammy Do you live by the Ten Commandments?

Rachel Six hundred and thirteen, it says here.

Josh (*to Tammy*) Why is everything a joke?

Tammy I'm not joking!

Josh Well, it certainly sounded like one.

Tammy I was just wondering if you covet your neighbour's ox?

Rachel Six hundred and thirteen laws. If you were to stick to every one of those, you'd never have to take responsibility for your actions. You don't want to live like that, do you, Josh?

Josh Who says I want to live like that, Mum?

Rachel Isn't that what this is all about?

Josh Some of it makes sense, and some of it doesn't. You just do what you can.

Danny When it's all laid down, Josh, it stops you asking questions.

Josh This is me you're talking about, Dad. When have I ever not asked questions? I'm always asking questions. That's why I'm always reading.

Tammy Yes, but now you're looking for simple answers.

Josh Am I?

Tammy Well, are you?

Josh Are *you*?

Tammy I'm still asking questions.

Josh Like what?

Tammy Like . . . let's pick the mother of all questions – why are we here?

Josh Why are we here – why are you here?

Tammy Oh, I'm here to change the world.

Josh Oh, yeah?

Tammy Seriously . . . you're here for a short time on earth, you do your bit, do your best. You leave your spirit behind, and you hope the world's a better place for it.

Danny That's why I still take NHS work. That's my bit.

Tammy And obviously, I'm here to make your life a living hell, Josh.

Josh Well, you're certainly doing that. You think you've got all the answers, don't you, Tammy? You sit there in your little Tammy world, and everything's hunky-dory!

Danny Josh – please!

Tammy Yeah, except my world's five hours behind your world, so I'm playing catch-up right now.

Rachel She's only making a joke, Josh.

Josh It's not funny, Mum.

Tammy Life's funny.

Danny Life . . . you've got to start living, Josh.

Rachel You can't sort out all the answers, and then go into the world. You've got to get out there and ask the questions, and then maybe you'll find some answers. If there are any.

Danny You're a logical man – you've got a rational mind. You've spent your life asking rational questions, and now, suddenly –

Rachel Now you've got yourself involved in something completely irrational.

Danny Exactly.

Josh (*shouting*) IT'S MY CHOICE!

Danny Oh, please don't shout.

Rachel Calm down, Josh – we're just trying to have a conversation.

Danny And every time we talk about something you don't agree with, you fly off the handle.

Josh If it gives me something, why can't you just accept it?

Rachel We can accept it. We're not criticising you, we're just talking about it.

Danny Why are you so angry?

Josh Because it's like the fucking Spanish Inquisition in here!

Rachel D'you know who you remind me of when you carry on like that?

Josh Who do I remind you of, Mum?

Tammy Groucho Marx.

Rachel Michelle. Your Auntie Mash. She'd get all defensive if you asked her a question she didn't like – she'd start screaming and shouting, 'fucking' this, 'fucking' that –

Josh storms out and slams the door.

– and then she'd storm out of the room and slam the door!

Tammy *L'chaim.* (*Pause.*) He's very scared.

Rachel We're all scared.

Danny (*simultaneously*) We're all scared.

Tammy gets up and wanders over to the bookshelf.

Tammy Have you got my *Rough Guide to Spain*? (*She goes over to Rachel.*) Come on, guys, it'll be alright.

Tammy and Rachel hold hands for a moment. Danny is holding up a small feather from a cushion.

Danny See this feather? It reminds me of Josh when he was a kid.

Rachel Why?

Danny The way he used to look at things for hours. Remember? Stones . . . clouds . . .

Tammy Yeah . . . and the way the sunlight hit the wall.

Danny Yeah. And I used to do my dog.

34

He makes a dog shadow-puppet with his hand.

Tammy Oh, your dog that looked like a hand.

Danny Oh!

Tammy Okay, when I was four, it looked like a dog, Dad!

Danny Thank you.

Tammy Yeah, it's a shame he could never share it with anyone, really.

She moves to the conservatory.

Rachel Close the door, will you, Tammy? It's getting chilly in here.

Tammy closes the conservatory doors.

Tammy You, er, got any new jokes, Dad? Come on, I've been away for two weeks – you must have a new joke for me.

Pause.

Danny Alright. I've got a joke. (*Pause.*) Four men, standing on a street corner. An American, a Russian, a Chinaman and an Israeli. And a man comes up to them and says, 'Excuse me, but what is your opinion of the meat shortage?' (*Pause.*) So . . . the American goes, 'What's a shortage?' The Russian goes, 'What is meat?' The Chinaman goes, 'What is an opinion?' And the Israeli goes, 'WHAT IS EXCUSE ME?!'

They all laugh.

Tammy Dad! That's bang out of order!

Danny Well, you know me and PC!

Tammy collects up her carrier bag and things.

Tammy Come on, *chaverim*, let's do the washing up.

She goes out to the kitchen. Rachel and Danny follow her, embracing briefly as they go. Fade to blackout.

SCENE EIGHT

Lights up. Saturday 7 May 2005. Afternoon. Another bright day. The conservatory doors are open.
   Josh is standing in the corner of the room. He is still wearing his skull-cap.
   Enter Danny, followed by Dave and Rachel.

Dave It's a bleeding *mishigas*, this parking business. Saturday afternoon, it's like a bloody car park out there; and when you do find a space, you need a taxi to get here from where you parked your car!

Danny So where did you park the car?

Dave Miles away – up by the school somewhere, I don't know.

Danny So where is Naomi?

Rachel She's tired. She didn't want to come.

Dave She woke up this morning, said she didn't feel like getting out of bed. I said, 'Alright, leave it till lunchtime, see how you feel.' So she gets up, has a bit of lunch, went back to bed. She says she's sorry, she didn't feel up to it.

Rachel I'll phone her later.

Dave No, don't. You'll wake her up, she's *shluffing*.

Rachel So I'll wait a bit.

Dave It's ridiculous. Last time I came round, I parked right outside the house.

Rachel That was over a year ago, Dad.

Dave Next time, you can stand outside and save me a parking space.

Rachel Next time, maybe you'll let one of us come and pick you up, like we offered.

Dave I don't need picking up, thank you very much. I'm perfectly capable of driving the car. I've been driving since 1946. All I need is somewhere to park the bloody thing.

Rachel Well park your *tuchus* down here, and stop *kvetching*. You've been doing that since 1946, as well. Next time, we'll get Danny to lie down in the road for you.

Dave has sat down.

Danny Oh, that's nice, Rachel – maybe you and I can lie down together!

Rachel sits on the sofa.

Dave Get Josh to lie down on the road – make a bigger space. Where is Josh, anyway?

Danny He's right here, Dave.

Dave Oh, is he? (*He looks round.*) Oh yes – I didn't see him skulking around in the corner there. So what's the matter, you don't say hello to your grandpa when he arrives?

Josh I'm sorry. I was just waiting for you to finish your utterly riveting conversation about the state of parking in Cricklewood. Hello, Grandpa.

Dave A *chochem, noch.* Clever bugger. So, what you been up to, eh? Here, what's he got on his head? He's wearing a *capple*? Is he wearing a *capple*? Oi, Josh! Are you wearing a *capple*?

Josh Yes Grandpa, I'm wearing a *capple*.

Dave starts to laugh.

Dave What, he's a *frummer*, all of a sudden? I don't believe it.

His laughter grows, and then turns into a cough. This develops further into a bad coughing attack. He takes out a handkerchief.

Rachel Here we go . . .

Danny Have you got your inhaler, Dave?

Eventually the attack subsides.

Rachel Alright?

Danny (*Yiddish*) Oy . . .

Having got over his coughing attack, Dave takes out a packet of cigarettes.

Rachel Oh, that's right! First your inhaler, then your cigarettes – what could be better?

Danny It loosens the phlegm.

He goes out.

Dave He's right – it loosens the phlegm.

Rachel Dad, emphysema is a smoker's disease – how can you possibly say it helps?

Dave Emphysema is not a smoker's disease – I've told you before, it's got nothing to do with it. Anyway, I'm seventy-eight years old, I've been smoking all my life, and I don't need lectures from you about smoking.

Danny returns with a large ashtray.

Danny Is this ashtray big enough for you, Dave?

Dave It'll do.

38

Danny joins Rachel on the sofa.

Danny So did Naomi get out to vote?

Dave Of course she voted.

Rachel I told you.

Dave We both voted. We always vote – you know that.

Danny What, she wasn't too tired?

Dave She's tired today. That was Thursday, she wasn't tired Thursday – what are you talking about?

Rachel He's only asking, Dad.

Dave Not that it makes any bloody difference.

Danny What, you voted Tory?

Dave Don't be ridiculous!

Danny Well, you never know.

Dave Blair, the Tories, it's all the same.

Rachel Oh, come on, Dad, I wouldn't go that far.

Danny They might be New Labour, but they're Labour.

Dave Labour? What's that mean these days?

Danny Well, they're still socialists.

Dave Socialists my arse! Blair's in bed with big business even more than the Tories now. When did this government ever do anything to hinder the City? Look at the millions they poured into his election campaign. I tell you, the Labour Party doesn't need trade union money any more – that's a piss in the ocean. There's no political party that represents us any more, the working people – it doesn't exist. No wonder half the electorate didn't bother to vote.

Danny Well, you can't argue with that.

Dave What about him? What did he vote?

Danny Well, he's sitting right there – why don't you ask him?

Josh Who's 'he'?

Dave You, my grandson. Who did you vote for?

Josh I don't wish to divulge that information, if you don't mind.

Dave What, highly classified, is it?

Josh What, so I'm supposed to tell you who I voted for?

He gets up.

Dave No, we're having a political discussion, the General Election was two days ago; surely you must have an opinion, don't you? Rabbi?

Josh Yes, I've got an opinion, and I'm not a rabbi.

Dave More's the pity. You should consider it – you might make a bob or two for the first time in your life.

Rachel Shut up, Dad.

Dave No, I mean it. It's a good number, being a rabbi – they make a bloody fortune.

Rachel Why are we talking about rabbis, all of a sudden? Anyway, it's not a number, it's a vocation.

Dave A vocation? Do me a favour. They're a bunch of crooks – it's like the Mafia.

Danny There are rabbis and rabbis.

Dave Whose side are you on? I don't believe what I'm hearing from you two. He's sprauncing around wearing a *capple*, and you're defending rabbis. What's going on in this house?

Danny I'm not defending rabbis.

Rachel I don't know why we're talking about rabbis in the first place.

Dave I'll tell you one thing, though. When I kick the bucket, you'll have your own personal rabbi on tap to say *Kaddish* for me for nothing. That's right isn't it, Josh? You wouldn't charge your own family, would you?

Rachel Anyway, I thought you didn't want a Jewish funeral.

Dave I don't, but the way things are looking here, I won't have much say in the matter, will I?

Josh Well, at least it'll be a quiet affair, 'cos you won't be there.

> *Josh leaves the room, and goes upstairs.*
> *Pause.*

Dave So, what? He's become a proper *frummer*, already?

Rachel It depends what you mean by *frummer*.

Dave Does he go to *shul*?

Danny No.

Dave So, what does he do, then?

Danny He gets up at seven o'clock every morning, and says his prayers in the conservatory.

Dave (*indicating his left arm*) Does he put on *tefillin*?

Danny No. No *tefillin*.

Rachel He's stopped eating bacon and ham, and he won't mix meat and milk.

Danny Oh, and he lights the candles every Friday night.

Dave What? *He* lights the candles? A man?

Rachel He asked me to do it, and I said no, so he does it himself.

Dave Bloody hell. How long's this been going on?

Danny A while.

Rachel Since last year.

Danny Confusing, isn't it?

Dave You can say that again.

Danny Yeah, for us, too.

Dave Confusing? It's more than confusing – it's bloody weird. He's lost his marbles!

Rachel Look, Dad. He's not doing anybody any harm.

Danny No.

Dave It's outrageous. He's a twenty-nine-year-old man.

Rachel He's twenty-eight, actually.

Dave Alright, twenty-eight. He's a twenty-eight-year-old man, and he's living off his parents. Well, isn't he?

Rachel It's hard for us, Dad.

Dave Hard? Yes, I'm sure it's hard. But I'll tell you something, if you don't mind my saying so. You make it hard for yourselves.

Pause.
Danny gets up.

Danny D'you fancy a spin round the garden, Dave?

Dave No, I'll have a cup of tea first.

Rachel Is that a hint, Dad?

The front door can be heard opening.

Tammy (*off*) Hiya!

Rachel Tammy's here. I'll put the kettle on.

She gets up. Enter Tammy.

Tammy Hi, Mum.

Rachel Hi.

They kiss.

Tammy Hi, Dad.

Danny Hello, darling.

They kiss.

Tammy Grandpa!

Dave Hello, *tchutchela*.

They kiss. Rachel goes out.

Tammy How's tricks?

Dave Alright. How's the United Nations?

Tammy Oh, I wish. Kofi Annan says hi, by the way. Yeah, he's sorry he can't make it – he's stuck in traffic on the A41.

Dave chuckles.

So where's Grandma?

Dave I left her at home with the gardener.

Tammy What, is he watering her plants?

Dave She was feeling a bit tired today.

Tammy Is she alright?

Dave Yes, she's fine.

Tammy Are you alright, Grandpa?

Dave Alright on one side.

Tammy Did you drive here?

Dave Of course – why shouldn't I?

Tammy 'Cos you're a danger to pedestrians and cyclists.

Dave Oh, is that so?

Rachel returns. Tammy has put her keys on a table.

Danny Tammy! How many times do I have to tell you – not on the table, please! It's bad luck!

He takes the keys out to the hall.

Tammy Oh, Dad, don't hang them up! Every time you hang them up, I forget to take them with me!

Danny (*off*) I'll remind you.

Tammy (*to Rachel*) He'll forget.

Rachel So what have you been up to this week, Tammy?

Tammy I've been working at the Royal Courts of Justice.

Rachel Doing what?

Tammy It's an insurance claim. A Spanish woman was in a car accident in St Albans. Anyway, I can't really talk about it – the case is still ongoing. I'm back in court on Monday.

Danny returns, and sits down.

Danny Sub judice.

Tammy Exactly, I wouldn't want to be a Judas!

Dave So you translate for her while her barrister is pleading her case. Is that right?

Tammy That is correct. First, I tell her what they're saying. And then I tell them what she's saying, 'cos that is what we do, we freelance interpreter people!

44

Dave What happens what she's being cross-examined?

Tammy Ah, well, then it goes both ways. That's what we call 'retour'.

Dave Sounds a bit complicated to me.

Tammy *Si, es muy complicado.*

Danny That's why you're not an interpreter, Dave.

Tammy *No, tu eres* grandpa.

Rachel Or a barrister.

Tammy Claire's going out with a barrister.

Danny Really?

Tammy Yeah – Dominic.

Dave Claire. Who's Claire?

Tammy My flatmate. She's a friend from Habonim. I was on Israel Tour with her.

Dave Oh yeah? So how come you didn't nab the barrister first?

Tammy We can't both have him. We share loo rolls – we can't share blokes as well.

Rachel Anyway, Dad, maybe Tammy's got a boyfriend of her own.

Danny Yes. Anything to report on that particular front, Tamara?

Rachel Something you might want to tell us?

Tammy Maybe, maybe not.

Rachel Sounds intriguing.

Josh has entered, and is standing by the conservatory door.

Josh You alright, Tammy?

Tammy Yeah, are you alright, Josh?

Rachel Anybody ready for that cup of tea?

Danny Oh, yes please!

Dave About bloody time.

Tammy D'you want me to give you a hand, Mum?

Rachel No, it's alright.

Tammy Are you sure?

Rachel Yes.

She goes out.

Dave So . . . what d'you think of your brother becoming a *frummer*, eh?

Tammy I wish him well to wear it.

Josh Thank you.

He sits on the sofa.

Tammy So did you vote BNP then, Grandpa?

Dave Of course, I always do. I campaigned for them – you know that.

Tammy Yeah, yeah – sure.

Danny Did you read today, Tam, the BNP came third in Barking.

Tammy Yeah, well, they're barking in Barking.

Danny No, don't joke, darling. They got sixteen point nine per cent of the vote. It's serious.

Tammy It is, I know.

Danny Yes, well . . .

Dave It's immaterial. Anyway, you don't need the BNP any more, you've got the Tory Party.

Danny You just said the Tories and the Labour Party were the same thing.

Dave No, no, no, what I was saying was, that the whole political spectrum has shrunk. There's no choice any more. That's why youngsters like Tammy are disenchanted with the whole process.

Tammy Who says I'm disenchanted? Disappointed, maybe, but I'm not disenchanted – I've still got hope.

Dave I'm pleased to hear it. What about your brother?

Danny You're doing it again! He's sitting right here – why don't you ask him?

Dave I'm asking him.

Josh Are you?

Dave Yes. Do you agree with your sister?

Josh About what?

Dave Do you still have hope? Do you believe in the political process in this country?

Josh Are you asking me or are you telling me?

Dave I'm asking you.

Josh Now, at what point in that conversation did you say, 'Josh, what's your opinion?'

Dave Never mind the bloody formalities, I'm asking you. Do you believe in the political process, or, now that you've found God and the rabbis, are you happy for them to take care of everything for us, like they did with the Holocaust?

Rachel has come into the room briefly, to put a cake on the table.

Rachel Dad!

She goes out. Josh gets up.

Josh Let's get to the point, Grandpa. What d'you want to talk about?

Tammy He wants to talk about Arsenal.

Josh Shut up, Tammy!

Dave I want to talk about you.

Josh What about me?

Dave For a start, I want to know why you're walking around ostentatiously with that piece of crap on your head.

Josh Why d'you want to know?

Dave 'Cos you're my grandson.

Josh And what's that got to do with it?

Dave How come a scientifically minded university graduate, brought up in a respectable secular household, turns to God?

Rachel has returned with the rest of the tea things. She and Tammy now start handing round tea and cake.

Josh And how come you've become so bigoted?

Dave I'm not the bigot!

Rachel Dad . . .!

Josh You were just talking about political choice. This is my choice.

Dave And you're entitled to your choice.

Josh Thank you.

Dave But that's not an explanation.

Josh Why not?

Dave Why not? Why not? Well, you could choose to go about on all fours. You could choose to chop up old ladies with an axe. You could choose to have *motzah* balls for breakfast. But what I'm looking for is a sensible answer to a legitimate question: why?

Rachel That's enough, Dad! Why d'you always have to go on the attack?

Dave I'm not on the attack.

Rachel Yes, you are on the attack.

Dave No, I'm not. I'm just trying to have a rational conversation with your son.

Rachel But it isn't a conversation, is it? It's a confrontation, like it always is with you.

Josh It's alright, Mum.

Rachel Just let it go.

Josh If he wants to have a conversation, let's have a conversation!

Dave At last! So – *nu*?

Tammy (*handing Danny some tea and cake*) Dad.

Danny (*quietly*) Thanks, darling.

Josh Does it affect your life in any way?

Dave Of course it does.

Josh How?

Dave Because rational discussion is what makes society work.

Josh (*shouting*) You're not answering the question!

Danny Josh, please!

Rachel Dad, when was the last time you had a rational discussion?

Danny With anyone?

Josh You're just changing the subject!

Dave Let me tell you something, Rachel. When we were on the kibbutz, all decisions were arrived at by a process of rational deliberation. Everyone was entitled to their opinion. You were listened to, you were questioned, you were interrogated. You were made to explain not just what your position was, but why you held to that position. Sometimes the discussions could go on all night. They were wonderful. They were stimulating. We thrived on argument, we thrived on debate. And, usually, with a bit of luck, by breakfast time a collective decision had been arrived at.

Rachel A collective decision.

Dave Of course – that's what rational discussion's all about.

Rachel But there was no scope for individual choice – everybody had to conform.

Dave Excuse me, Rachel. Have you never heard of democracy?

Rachel Don't patronise me, Dad. I'm talking about personal choice. Look: on the kibbutz, every aspect of people's lives was regulated by the General Assembly, and people were often scared to express an opinion, because they didn't want to be made to feel like outsiders.

Dave Rubbish! They always expressed their opinions – you couldn't shut them up, bloody *kibbutzniks*! Listen,

Rachel: personal choice without explanation is dangerous. That's where fascism begins. Hitler made personal choices, and look what happened.

Danny What, if he'd explained them, it wouldn't have happened?

Dave But he didn't explain them, did he? That's the whole bloody point!

Danny What difference?

Dave There's a world of difference!

Rachel He had a whole bloody army!

Dave Exactly. He had the whole German army at his disposal. So he didn't need to explain anything, did he? Strength has nothing to do with reason.

Josh Grandpa, let me ask you a question.

Dave What?

Josh Are you proud to be Jewish?

Dave What sort of a question's that?

Josh It's a straightforward question with a straightforward answer.

Dave You're born Jewish. You are as you are. I'm proud of some things, and not so proud of others.

Josh So what are you ashamed of?

Dave Ashamed?

Josh Yeah.

Pause.

Dave Yeah, I'll tell you what I'm ashamed of. I'm ashamed of Jewish racists. They should know better. Their grandparents came to this country as immigrants themselves, for God's sake. I was ashamed of all those Jewish arse-lickers in Margaret Thatcher's Cabinet. And, I'm afraid to say, I'm ashamed of what's happened to Israel. I'm ashamed of the Lebanon War; I'm ashamed of the illegal settlements on the West Bank and in Gaza; I'm ashamed of the way they treat the Palestinian people –

Tammy You mean you're ashamed of the Zionist state?

Dave No, no, no, Tammy, don't put words in my mouth. I'm not ashamed of the Zionist state. I'm ashamed of the way Zionism has been hijacked by a bunch of right-wing religious nutters.

Pause.

Tammy Yeah . . . isn't etymology fascinating? I mean, the way words evolve. Take the word Zionism, for example. Once upon a time, it meant something positive and hopeful. But now . . . well, to some people it's a dirty word.

Rachel Yes, but even fifty or sixty years ago it was a dirty word to the Palestinians.

Dave And to the British, excuse me.

Tammy Yeah, for sure.

Josh Let me ask you another question, Grandpa.

Dave What?

Josh What does it mean to you to be Jewish?

Dave What does it mean? I'll tell you what it means. It means visiting your family for a couple of hours on a Saturday afternoon, and finding yourself in the middle of a fucking war zone. That's what it means.

Rachel Well, it should be a home from home for you then, Dad, shouldn't it?

Dave What're you talking about?

Rachel Don't you remember Friday nights at Sunny Hill? Everybody screaming and shouting, running up and down stairs, slamming doors; Mum with a face as long as a fiddle, Michelle storming out of the house, and disappearing for twenty-four hours? That was a war zone!

Dave That's a load of bollocks, and you know it.

Rachel It's how I remember it.

Dave No wonder Mash hasn't been in touch with you for God knows how many years.

Rachel She hasn't been in touch with any of us for God knows how many years, has she?!

Dave Well, don't shout at me, Rachel!

Rachel I'm not shouting at you!

Dave Yes, you are shouting at me!

Rachel I'm sorry then!

Dave That's alright!

Tammy Kofi Annan's going to be really sorry he missed this.

Josh Okay, Tammy, what does it mean to you to be Jewish?

Tammy Me?

Josh Yes, you.

Tammy Well, being Jewish is just part of who I am.

Josh What's that supposed to mean?

Tammy Well, like my little toe . . . or my middle finger. It's not the whole of me – I feel Jewish, and I don't feel Jewish. And I've got no idea what it's like not to be Jewish.

Josh What, so it doesn't have any meaning? It doesn't have any resonance?

Dave What d'you want her to do, rabbi? Wear a *sheitl* on her head, and go to the *mikvah* to cleanse her sins?

Dave starts an angina attack.

Josh (*shouting*) For the last time, I'm not a bloody rabbi!

Danny (*shouting*) And for the last time, Josh, will you stop shouting?! I'm sick of it!

Dave is taking a pill. Tammy rushes out to the kitchen. Rachel has gone over to Dave.

Rachel Have you taken a pill, Dad?

Dave Yes, I've taken one.

Danny Tammy –?

Tammy rushes in with a glass of water.

Tammy Coming, Dad! There's some water, Grandpa.

Dave sips the water.

Danny (*quietly*) Drink it slowly.

Rachel You bring this on yourself, Dad. You really do.

Danny Have some more. Now, sit back.

Dave I don't want to sit back.

Danny looks at Rachel, shrugs and walks away from Dave.

Rachel Is it easing off a bit now, Dad?

Dave Yes. It's easing off.

Rachel Are you alright?

Dave Yeah, I'm alright.

He starts getting up.

Rachel Where are you going now?

Dave I need a bloody piss.

Rachel D'you want Danny to go up with you?

Dave is heading for the door.

Dave Don't be stupid! What d'you want him to do? Unzip me flies, and get me bloody *shmackel* out for me? (*He stops.*) Go on, Josh. Give us a smile. I'm not dead yet. Rabbi! (*He continues out of the room.*) Why can't you get a bloody downstairs toilet here? I've been telling you for years.

Dave goes upstairs. Josh goes into the garden.

Rachel Go upstairs with him for me, Danny!

Danny You heard what he just said.

Rachel Please.

Danny Alright.

Rachel Thank you.

Danny goes upstairs. Rachel and Tammy start clearing the tea things.

Rachel So . . . ?

Tammy Yeah, I know what you're gonna ask me.

Rachel What?

Tammy 'So, who is he?'

Rachel Something like that.

Tammy Where to begin . . . ?

Rachel Well, I don't want to sound like a Jewish mother or anything, but, er – what's his name? How old is he? What does his father do? And what's his blood group?

Tammy Blood group O. Name, Tzachi.

Rachel Tzachi? Where's he from?

Tammy Israel.

Rachel That's nice.

They get on with clearing up the tea things. Fade to blackout.

Act Two

Lights up. Saturday 3 September 2005. Afternoon. Bright sunlight. The conservatory doors are open. So is the door into the hall.
    The room is empty.
    Pause.
    The sound of a key in the front door, which then opens.

Tammy (*off*) Hiya!

    Tammy enters. She is carrying her shoulder bag. She is followed by Tzachi, who is carrying a carrier bag.

Hello! (*She looks around.*) The abandoned fortress.

Tzachi Very nice.

Tammy Yeah, Mum and Dad must be picking up Grandpa. This is it. This is where it all kicked off. A conducted tour. This is the living room. That's the library. (*She goes over to the bookshelf.*) This is where she received her education. This is the sofa.

Tzachi Oh, really?

Tammy Yeah. This is where she received her further education. And that's it. The next tour's in an hour.

    She sits on the end of the sofa.

Tzachi So where is your brother?

Tammy He's probably in his room.

Tzachi You want to say hello to him?

Tammy He might be asleep!

She puts her arms round him.

Tzachi What are you doing? I cannot kiss you in your father's house.

Tammy Oh, yeah – you're probably right.

She pulls him down to her and kisses him. This develops into a full-scale snog. Rachel comes in from the garden, carrying a newspaper. She watches them for a few moments. Then Tammy sees her, and laughs.

Mum! Hello!

Rachel You look surprised to see me.

She puts down the newspaper.

Tammy Mum, this is Tzachi – Tzachi this is my mum, Rachel.

Rachel Hello.

She shakes his hand.

Tzachi Hi.

Rachel *Shalom. Ma shlomchah?*

Tzachi *Yofi. Ma nishmah?*

Rachel *Tov, todah.*

Tzachi Very good!

Rachel Hello, you!

Tammy Hi, Mum.

They hug and kiss.

Rachel You look wonderful!

Tammy Thanks. So do you.

Rachel Thanks.

Tammy Yeah, we had a great holiday – didn't we?

Tzachi Yes. Very good. Very good.

Rachel Come in. Sit down. Don't be shy.

Rachel sits in the armchair. Tammy and Tzachi sit on the sofa.

Tammy So is Dad picking up Grandpa?

Rachel Yes, they shouldn't be too long. So d'you want a cold drink, you two?

Tammy Yeah, yeah – d'you want anything?

Tzachi shrugs.

D'you want something, Mum? (*She gets up.*)

Rachel No, thank you. Tammy, take, erm –

Tammy Tzachi.

Rachel Tzachi's jacket, and hang it up for him.

Tammy takes off her own jacket, relieves Tzachi of his, and goes out.

Rachel So you enjoyed your holiday, Tzachi?

Tzachi Yes . . . very good. Very good.

Rachel You been there before, Spain?

Tzachi For me is, er, first time. In Europe.

Rachel Well, how long have you been in London?

Tzachi A year. Nearly.

Rachel 'Cos your English is good.

Tzachi It's okay.

Rachel It's fine!

Tzachi Slowly.

Rachel Whereabouts in Israel are you from?

Tzachi A kibbutz. In the north.

Tammy enters with two glasses of water.

Tammy I hope you haven't told her everything.

Rachel Only the naughty bits.

Tammy That can't have taken long.

She sits next to Tzachi on the sofa.

Rachel It's very nice to see you both.

Tammy Thanks.

Pause.

Tzachi I'm very sorry . . . for your loss.

Rachel Thank you.

Pause.

Tammy Yeah, I was asking Tzachi why he thought Jews always wished each other a long life after someone had died. Go on, tell her what you said.

He shakes his head.

Go on – tell her.

Tzachi Because . . . we are masochists.

Pause.

Tammy So how's Grandpa doing?

Rachel He's alright. He thinks he's better than he is. He shuffles off every day to get his paper and a few odds and ends, and . . . then he comes back to an empty house. And sits. He's very lonely.

Tammy Sure.

Rachel I go round there every other day, on Fridays I take him to Sainsburys, and that's it. And I worry about him. I worry about him going upstairs every night on his own – his breathing isn't at all good.

Tammy Have you heard from Mash yet?

Rachel No, and neither has he, and he's heartbroken about it. And furious with her, understandably, although I keep telling him I don't think she can know.

Tammy shrugs.

Well, you shrug, and your dad does the same, but I can't believe that Michelle, with all her selfishness, and all her madnesses, wouldn't get in touch with her family if she knew her mother had died. You know about my sister?

Tzachi Yes . . .

Tammy Yeah, I've told him all about our genetic malfunctions.

Rachel Families!

Tzachi It's the same everywhere.

Tammy So how's Josh?

Rachel Josh is . . . Josh. He's upstairs.

Tammy Tzachi's got a brother.

Tzachi Yes, also he's, er, older than me.

Rachel Is he in Israel?

Tzachi Yes. A little town near Haifa.

Tammy He's an archaeologist.

Rachel Really? Well, it's a good place to be an archaeologist.

Tzachi He keeps our mother and father happy.

Rachel Because he stayed in Israel?

Tzachi Israel; working; archaeologist . . .

Rachel They'd probably prefer it if he, and you, too, I'm sure, were on the kibbutz with them.

Tzachi For them, yes, is difficult. My grandfather was a *chalutz*, a pioneer, one of the founders of the kibbutz –

The doorbell rings. Rachel gets up.

Rachel Excuse me. *Slicha.*

She goes out. The following moments of Tammy and Tzachi are intimate, tactile, sexy and virtually inaudible.

Tzachi Very good.

Tammy *Ma ha-shaah?*

Tzachi *Reva le'arbah.*

Tammy So what time should we leave?

Tzachi Don't know. What time does it start?

Tammy Six-thirty.

Tzachi When d'you want to leave?

Tammy We can leave a bit earlier.

Tzachi Okay.

Tammy Shall we eat afterwards?

Tzachi Yes.

Tammy I think that's my brother.

The following exchange in the hall runs simultaneously with the above, and is reasonably audible.

Rachel I thought you were upstairs.

Josh I was. I went out for a walk, forgot my fucking keys.

Rachel There's no need to swear about it. Your sister's here.

Josh So?

Rachel She's got her boyfriend with her.

Josh Her what?

Rachel Her boyfriend – come and say hello.

She comes back into the room, followed by Josh.

Rachel This is Josh, Tammy's brother. This is –

Tzachi Tzachi.

Rachel I'm sorry, Tzachi. (*to Tammy*) He left his keys behind.

Josh So, you're an Israeli?

Tzachi Er, yes.

Josh 'Tzachi.' What does that mean?

Tzachi It's from the Bible, short for Itzchak.

Tammy Isaac.

Josh I know.

Tzachi Avraham and Sarah . . . they are very old. They don't have baby. They ask God for this. After a long time, Sarah, she has a little baby. She is very happy. So she laughs. Avraham sees this, so he calls the baby Itzchak, which means 'laughter'.

Josh So, you're a comedian, then?

Tammy It's a very long story for a very short name.

Rachel It's a good story.

Josh Fascinating. I'm just going to get a glass of water.

He goes out.

Rachel Sit down, Tzachi.

Tammy Yeah, you were saying about your grandfather.

Tzachi Yes. He started the kibbutz . . . so, er, for my mother, she is his daughter. Also, for my father –

Tammy Yeah, but you can't live out someone else's dream for them.

Josh hovers in the doorway with a glass of water.

Rachel How many of the kids from your class stayed on the kibbutz?

Tzachi From my class, three.

Rachel Out of how many?

Tzachi Thirty-five, more or less.

Rachel Three out of thirty-five? It's nothing.

Tzachi The kibbutz now is, er, for old people.

Rachel The very old and the very young.

Tzachi Yes, also for children is perfect – for me it was great when I was little. Now, it's . . .

Rachel Sure.

Pause.

Tzachi (*to Josh*) You've been on kibbutz?

Josh I visited one once. Why?

Tzachi Like it?

Josh No, not really.

Tammy Everybody visited kibbutzim, on Israel Tour, with Habonim. It's a rite of passage thing you do when you're sixteen.

Rachel You go as a volunteer for six weeks or so, but the kids on the kibbutz didn't mix much with the volunteers, did they?

Tammy No, they saw it as a foreign invasion.

Tzachi The grown-ups saw it as a foreign invasion.

Rachel They saw us as spoilt Jewish bourgeois kids, who were a bad influence on their children. And then there were the volunteers from the rest of the world, who were mostly not Jewish, and they had a problem with them, as well.

Tzachi Yes, the mothers were afraid the Swedish *shiksa* girls would steal away their Jewish boys.

Rachel And the other way around.

Tzachi laughs.

So, what, then you went into the army?

Tzachi Yes.

Josh So, you were in the army?

Tzachi Everybody.

Tammy He was in tanks.

Josh Was it fun?

Tzachi (*laughing*) No, it was, er . . . boring. Near Lebanon, the border. A lot of sitting around, doing nothing.

Josh Something I know all about.

Rachel So you two met in New York, I hear?

This question induces much mirth and amusement in Tammy and Tzachi – a private joke of some sort.

Tammy Yeah, yeah, New York . . .

Rachel And you kept in touch ever since.

More amusement.

Tammy Kind of . . .

Pause.

So, how're things, Josh?

Josh What am I supposed to say to that?

Tammy Well, what – you been out?

Josh I went for a walk.

Tammy How was it?

Josh The sun's still shining.

Tammy Thank you, Bob Dylan!

Tzachi You are studying?

Josh I'm always studying. I study life.

Tzachi Big subject.

Tammy Tzachi did philosophy at university.

Rachel Where, at the Hebrew University?

Tzachi No, Tel-Aviv.

Josh Why d'you choose philosophy?

Tzachi (*laughing*) You really want to know?

Josh Yeah.

Tzachi (*laughing*) To piss off my mother and father!

Josh You chose a subject to piss off your parents?

Tzachi Also it is interesting for me, but also to, er – piss off my parents.

Rachel Because they wanted you to do something practical – am I right?

Tzachi Yes, er, Business Studies, Agricultural Management . . .

Josh So, did you learn anything? Anything you want to share with the masses?

Tzachi Only to bullshit.

Rachel And then you came to London to bullshit my daughter!

Tzachi Yeah, and it worked. And now we sit around all night, talking philosophical rubbish.

Josh That sounds like you.

Josh leaves, and goes upstairs.

Tammy He is a charmer!

Rachel (*to Tzachi*) I'm sorry. We try not to take any notice.

Pause.

Rachel So, Tzachi . . . are you working?

Tzachi Studying, working . . .

Rachel What are you studying? Where are you working?

Tzachi I study English; working in . . .

Tammy He photocopies in the City.

Tzachi Photocopy factory – lawyers, architects, plans, documents.

Tammy Near Liverpool Street.

Rachel Liverpool Street? And where d'you live?

Tzachi Swiss Cottage. Not far.

Rachel So you go to work on the tube?

Tzachi Yes.

Rachel So, Tzachi, you've been living in London for nearly a year, you travel to work every day on the tube, and suddenly find yourself in a horribly familiar situation, with bombs going off, on tubes and on buses; that must have come as a bit of a surprise to you!

Tzachi A surprise . . . no, I think we are always expecting a bomb, in London.

Rachel What, since the war in Iraq started?

Tzachi Before – nine-eleven, no?

Tammy Only now it's our turn; terrorism's landed in Good Old Blighty.

Tzachi What is, er –?

Tammy Old Blighty. It's a small group of islands off the French coast. The United Kingdom of Great Britain and Northern Ireland, also known as England. And now it's arrived, it's a wake-up call.

Rachel But terrorism hasn't just arrived in this country, Tammy. It's been here for years. I can remember the IRA bombings in London.

Tammy That was then, Mum. I'm talking about global terrorism – now that it's here, we've got a responsibility to deal with it.

Tzachi But we are dealing – people are doing!

Tammy Who?

Tzachi George Bush, Tony Blair . . .

Tammy That is exactly what I'm *not* talking about – they're not people! Look: two days after the Madrid bombings, the Spanish voted in a Socialist government.

Rachel We've only just had an election here, and, anyway, who are we going to change this lot for?

Tammy No, you're missing the point, Mum.

Rachel I'm sorry.

Tammy I'm talking about reactions to terrorism. In Spain, it was positive – here it was like completely negative.

Tzachi How negative?

Tammy Oh, deporting terror suspects to countries where they might be tortured, infringing on human rights and freedom of speech – oh, and let's shoot a Brazilian electrician for jumping over a turnstile in the London underground – which he didn't even jump over!

Tzachi No, no, this Brazilian guy is, er, a big mistake – is not a policy of a government.

Tammy No, because a soldier took a piss when he was meant to be watching a block of flats.

Tzachi (*overlapping*) Yes!

Rachel I think that's one man's negligence, it's not official government policy, Tammy.

Tammy I'm talking about aggressive reactions to terrorism, and the cycles of fear they cause.

Tzachi You must separate two things. In Spain, is the reaction of people; here, is the reaction of government.

Tammy Yeah, but the people should affect the reaction of the government.

Tzachi Yes.

Rachel If the bombings had happened before the election, the people would have affected the reaction of the government, and we'd have ended up with a Conservative government, in my opinion.

Tammy I'm talking about reacting to the violence *with* violence, and that just breeding *more* violence.

Tzachi You are always talking abstract. You need to deal in reality. If a man gets on a bus with a bomb, you have to shoot him – you have to kill him.

Tammy Oh, spoken like an Israeli in a tank!

Tzachi You always do this – you take what you like, you throw away what you don't like – you're not dealing in reality, you are being idealistic.

Tammy And what's wrong with having ideals? Anyway, hold on . . . we're having the same argument that we always have. (*She holds his hand.*) In a minute, he's going to compare me to Bush and Bin Laden.

She gets up and goes to the sideboard.

Tzachi (*to Rachel*) Bush . . . Bin Laden . . . they are dealing in propaganda, they are selective with the truth. You are idealistic also, you are being selective, it is very dangerous. Is all I'm saying.

Tammy has picked up a hardback book.

Tammy Okay. Guess what this is?

She places the book on her head, open, like a roof. Then she swings one arm like a pendulum, and makes a clock-ticking noise with her tongue, rolling her eyes from side to side. Then her tongue becomes a cuckoo, and she makes cuckoo chiming noises, as it pops out of her mouth a few times. In other words, she imitates a cuckoo clock.

Rachel D'you know what that is?

Tzachi Er . . .

Rachel That's my cuckoo daughter, that's what that is!

Tzachi laughs.

Tammy Yeah – one just flew over my nest! Present, Mum – from Majorca, from both of us.

She gives Rachel a plainly wrapped gift from the carrier bag Tzachi arrived with.

Rachel Thank you. Beautifully wrapped, as always. (*She unwraps it.*) Very nice. What is it?

Tammy It's an olive dish. You put the stone in the pot.

Rachel Oh, and the little cocktails sticks in there?

Tammy Yeah.

Rachel Very handy. Thank you. It's lovely.

She kisses Tammy.

Tammy Oh, it's a pleasure, Mum.

Danny and Dave can be heard arriving though the front door.

Danny (*off*) Hello!

Rachel (*to Tzachi*) I'm going to give you a kiss, as well. (*She does so.*)

Tammy (*in the doorway*) Hi, Dad!

Danny (*off*) Hello, darling!

Rachel (*to Tzachi*) Now the fun starts!

Enter Dave, followed by Danny.

Tammy Hello, Grandpa!

Rachel Alright, Dad?

Dave No, I'm not.

Tammy Yeah, it's good to see you, too. Grandpa – this is my friend Tzachi. Tzachi, this is Grandpa Dave; Grandpa Dave, this is Tzachi.

Dave Tzachi. Tzachi. Sounds Israeli. Are you Israeli?

Tzachi Er, yes!

Dave *Shalom. Ma shlomchah?*

Tzachi *Tov, todah. Ma mishmash?*

Dave *B'seder.* Rachel, come here . . .

The following runs inaudibly under the above, beginning after Dave: 'No, I'm not.'

Danny He's driving me mad – he says I was half-an-hour late!

Rachel You're not half-an-hour late.

Danny I know I'm not half-an-hour late.

Rachel Well, don't worry about it. Look. Look who's here.

Danny Is he nice?

Rachel He's very nice – you'll like him.

Danny D'you like him . . .?

During the following, Rachel arranges cushions for Dave.

Dave *B'seder.* Rachel, come here. Can you explain something to me, please?

Rachel What, Dad?

Dave How is it you tell me he's going to pick me up at three o'clock, he doesn't turn up till gone half past?

Rachel Dad, I said half past.

Dave You said three o'clock.

Rachel I said half past.

Dave No, you didn't, you said three o'clock. I sit there like a *shmock*, waiting for him. I can't even go in the garden because you can't hear the doorbell from the garden . . .

Rachel You forgot, Dad.

Dave I did not forget. Not only that. We could've been here half an hour ago, only this *chochem* of a husband of yours thinks he knows north-west London like the back of his hand.

Rachel Well, you're here now, Dad, so stop complaining!

Dave sits down.

Dave Look, it's simple: I live in Hendon, you live in Cricklewood. All he's got to do is cut across, go straight down the Edgware Road!

Danny I don't like going down the Edgware Road on a Saturday afternoon, there's too much traffic.

Dave Traffic? What're you talking about traffic?

Danny That's why I go down the Hendon Way – there's no traffic!

Dave So instead you do these *mishiginah* back-doubles?

Danny Are you calling the Hendon Way a back-double?

Dave Of course it's a back-double! You end up doing a bloody scenic tour of Golders Green. I thought he was taking me to Wembley Stadium, for Christ's sake!

*The following two sections of dialogue run quietly in
the doorway under different parts of the above.
Beginning after Dave: 'B'seder . . .'*

Tammy Hi, Dad. You alright?

Danny No, I'm not. He's driving me mad.

Tammy Dad, let me introduce you to my friend Tzachi.
This is my Dad, Danny; Danny, this is Tzachi.

Danny Tzachi?

Tzachi Yes.

Danny That's short for something, yes?

Tzachi Er, yes! Itzchak.

Danny Isaac?

Tzachi Yes.

Danny Isaac the Wise.

Tammy I told you, the man's a genius.

Danny Sit down, Tzachi. I'll talk to you in a minute.

Directly following Dave: 'Of course it's a back-double.'

Rachel Look what our daughter brought us.

Danny What is it?

Rachel It's for olives – you put the pips in there, and the
sticks in there –

Danny Very nice – we'll never use it.

Rachel You're right!

Dave has lit a cigarette.

Dave So, what? You're a kibbutznik or something?

Tzachi (*laughing*) I was.

Dave D'you know Kfar Hanassi?

Tzachi Yes, it is not far from my kibbutz.

Dave Kfar Hanassi was my kibbutz.

Tzachi Really?

Dave I went there on *Aliyah*. 1950. Did she tell you her mother was born on Kfar Hanassi, 1952?

Rachel sits on the sofa. Danny gives Dave an ashtray.

Rachel 1954, Dad!

Danny Give her a break, Dave!

Dave Uh. That's right. Yes, I was married there, 1952. My late wife . . . unfortunately . . .

Tzachi Yes, I am, er, sorry for your loss . . .

Dave (*overlapping*) . . . a couple of months ago . . . she passed away . . . (*Pause.*) She was from Liverpool, my wife, a Scouser. I was from London, she was from Liverpool. We met on the kibbutz, got married, and she's the result. There's another one as well, but who the bloody hell knows where she is? Kicking around somewhere, God knows.

Danny Is Josh upstairs?

Rachel Yeah.

Tzachi has taken out a cigarette.

Tzachi Is it okay if I, er . . .?

Danny Yes, of course.

Dave No, it is not okay. Believe you me, it is not okay. You take out a cigarette in this house, and straightaway they give you a song and dance, you wish to hell you'd never been born.

Danny goes to the kitchen for an ashtray.

Rachel No one's going to give him a song and dance, Dad – he hasn't got emphysema.

Dave Oh, don't start on again about emphysema, for Christ's sake, I've told you a million times, it's got nothing to do with it.

Tammy Tzachi's from Kibbutz Dalia, Grandpa.

Dave Dalia? Now, where's Dalia?

Tammy (*amused*) It's near Kfar Hanassi.

Pause.

Dave Dalia. That was started by the Romanians, wasn't it?

Tzachi Yes. Very good!

Danny returns with an ashtray.

Danny There you go.

Tzachi Thank you.

Pause.

Dave Funnily enough, a friend of mine from the East End went to Dalia. Cyril Nyman. D'you know the name Nyman?

Tzachi There was a family, Nyman. They left, to Tel-Aviv.

Dave I don't suppose he's still alive any more. God knows why he ever went to Dalia. Couldn't speak a word of Romanian. He was a very funny fellow, Cyril. He kept us entertained for a whole week on the boat. Marseille to Haifa. He had a ukulele. Of course, I was there before Independence, you know. Palestine. I was there with the British Army. 1947. End of the Mandate. Nice job for a Jewish boy from Stepney. Keeping out the Holocaust survivors. Poor buggers. You were in the army?

Tzachi Of course.

Danny I bet you've seen some things you'd rather not talk about.

Tzachi It was okay. A lot of smoking.

He mimes dope-smoking. Everyone is amused except Dave, who isn't listening. He is looking at his watch.

Dave You know, Rachel . . . if I kept appointments in my firm over the years like he keeps appointments, I'd have gone *mechullah* in six months, belly up.

Danny Dave, my whole life is about keeping appointments.

Dave You don't keep appointments. They keep appointments. They come to you and they open their mouths. What do you do? *Gurnisht.*

Danny Oh, that's right – nothing, of course!

Rachel He works very hard, Dad.

Dave Oh, yeah.

Tammy Tzachi used to work in removals, Grandpa.

Danny Really?

Dave Where?

Tzachi New York.

Rachel New York? That's exciting! You must've got to know the city really well, driving around everywhere.

Tzachi It was, er, crazy time.

Tammy Mm, crazy stories!

Dave I knew a fellow years ago . . . a Yiddisher fellow . . . what was his name? Used to play bridge with him. Bernie something . . . Anyway, he sold up, went to New York, started a firm doing removals for the ultra-orthodox *Yiddles* in Brooklyn there, the *ganzer frummers*. He's probably dead by now.

Tzachi The *meshugah frummers*, always shouting, never tipping – if you knock, or scratch the furniture, oy-oy-oy!

Rachel My father knows all about that, Tzachi, because he also used to move the *frummers* around, didn't you, Dad? He had them *plotzing* and praying all the way from Stamford Hill to Temple Fortune.

Dave Load of *momzers*. Never stopped complaining. Took months to pay their bills – you were lucky if you got paid. Always some excuse! If you were five minutes late . . . if you packed in one milk plate with the meat things . . . Ergh! It was bleedin' nightmare.

Danny It's a pity we didn't know Tzachi in those days, Dave. He could've taken over your business.

Dave He'd have been bloody welcome to it.

Danny Oh! Er, nuts, anyone?

He offers a bowl of pistachio nuts to Tammy.

Tammy (*taking some*) Oh, thanks, Dad.

Danny Go on, force yourself!

Tammy (*taking some more*) Thank you!

Danny (*offering*) Tzachi?

Tzachi takes some. Danny offers Rachel the nuts.

Rachel Not for me. I'm going to make some tea soon.

Danny Well, I know you don't want any, Dave. But I do. (*He takes some.*)

Dave Nah.

Pause.

So, what's going to happen with Israel now, after this Gaza business? Are they going to pull out of the West Bank?

Danny No, of course not.

Tzachi I don't think they were ever going to do this.

Danny No. Pulling out of Gaza was just a sop.

Rachel Anyway, half the families that have left Gaza are now moving to the West Bank.

Tzachi More people moved to the West Bank last year than were taken from Gaza now.

Tammy Yeah, well, forgive me for being idealistic, but I thought this might be the start of a real peace process.

Tzachi With Sharon, there is no peace process. There is only Israeli security.

Dave Never mind Sharon. Looks like they're going to elect that right-wing *potz* – whatsisname?

Danny Netanyahu.

Dave Yeah.

Tzachi And now they are finished with the pullout, it is go back to business as usual, in-fighting in the parliament, ego, not dealing with the real issue . . .

Tammy Yeah, well, a little birdie told me that Sharon might start his own party, and continue the peace process.

Rachel Yes, with Shimon Peres.

Danny What particular birdie was that, darling?

Tammy The *Guardian*.

Tzachi Yes, there is idea of Peres and Sharon together, but I don't think Sharon will leave the Likud – it's his party, he started it.

Danny But even if Peres and Sharon do form their own party, d'you think anyone's going to vote for them, two old men?

Tzachi Maybe.

Tammy What have you got to say to that, Grandpa?

Dave What are you talking about? The Israelis have always elected old men. Look at Ben-Gurion, look at Levi Eshkol, look at Menachim Begin, look at Golda Meir.

Danny Well, she wasn't an old man, was she?

Dave *Chochem*! (*to Tzachi*) Now what I want to know from you is, are they going to go on building that bloody wall?

Tzachi I don't think there is anybody, any mainstream politician, who wants to stop it.

Danny What, you think it's a good idea, the wall?

Tzachi It's not, er, good idea, bad idea. Is, er, does it stop the terrorists to get through? Does it stop the bomb? Yes!

Tammy But building a wall's a completely aggressive act.

Tzachi Okay, we are not talking about the Palestinians, we are talking about Israeli security.

Tammy Yeah, short-term security, not long-term security for everybody.

Tzachi (*laughing*) Welcome to Israel! In Israel, there is no long-term. You want long-term, you want maybe a viable, legitimate Palestinian state, but Israel make it very difficult – strategic settlements, roads connecting them to Israel, this breaks up the Palestinian land, it turn it into ghettoes.

Josh has drifted into the room. He gravitates towards the conservatory.

Danny Yes, but that's very short-sighted, Tzachi. All it does is, it polarises the two sides even further.

Rachel How can they be any more polarised than they already are?

Tammy Yeah, but there are Israelis and Palestinians working together for peace.

Rachel Only a minority, Tammy.

Tzachi The Palestinians make very many mistake. But their big mistake is suicide bomb. It make it very easy for Sharon to demonise, dehumanise the Palestinians. If they want their freedom, they need first of all, sort out corruption. Then the Palestinian people need to take responsibility, offer non-violent resistance to the occupation.

Rachel Yes, but even if they did that, there's always going to be a group of extremists who are committed to obliterating Israel.

Tammy But that's totally pessimistic.

Rachel The situation in the Middle East is pessimistic.

Tammy Cool! Let's all wallow in pessimism. Dad, get my keys – we might as well all go home!

Danny No, but seriously, Tammy, the question is, why is it pessimistic?

Tammy Because the end of the world is nigh, obviously.

Tzachi You are always idealistic again. In Israel it is the facts on the ground . . . a new settlement outpost, a suicide bomb, a *kasam* rocket on the settlers, you know, is a reaction to a reaction to a reaction. It never ends.

Dave So . . . you're a young Israeli, and you're saying there's no hope?

Tzachi Until the Palestinian leadership decides to stop help themselves, start help the people, I don't see hope.

Dave I see. So unless the poor bloody Palestinians find themselves a Mahatma Gandhi, the game's up.

Tzachi Maybe.

Rachel Yes, but the Israelis also need to find themselves a man of peace.

Danny Yeah. They need their own Mahatma Gandhi.

Tammy And the problem is, there are never enough Mahatma Gandhis to go around.

Rachel No. But they did have Yitzchak Rabin.

Danny Yep. Well . . .

Dave No, the short answer is: Israel needs a good kick up the arse from the Americans. But that's never going to happen, is it? 'Cos the Zionist lobby in the States has got the Administration by the balls.

Rachel Excuse me, Dad, but you're talking complete nonsense. The Americans do what the Americans want to do.

Dave Oh, so you know, do you? What, you've been over in Washington, having a chat with Condoleezza Rice, I suppose?

Rachel No, not this week – why, have you?

Danny Yeah, he's on the phone to her every night.

Dave I want to ask a question. Wouldn't it be nice, just once in a blue moon, I should get a proper greeting from my grandson when he sees me?

Rachel (*leaping up*) Does anybody want a cup of tea?

Danny (*leaping up*) Yes, please!

In the following passage, the dialogue sometimes overlaps and runs simultaneously, and is always loud. These are the separate segments:
Beginning after Rachel: 'Does anyone want a cup of tea?'

Tammy (*getting up*) Yeah, I'll help you, Mum. (*to Tzachi*) D'you want a cup of tea? Listen, if my Dad asks you to open your mouth, don't panic!

She follows Rachel out to the kitchen.
Beginning after Dave: '. . . since poor Grandma died.'

Danny Tzachi, I'd like to talk to you about avocados.

Tzachi Er, okay . . .

Danny D'you know anything about avocados?

Tzachi We grow them on Dalia, but –

Danny Good, because I'd like to ask your advice.

Dave Danny, DANNY!

Danny Yes, what is it, Dave?

Etc. See below in 3. for the rest of the above dialogue.
Beginning after Rachel: 'Does anybody want a cup of tea?'
This is really a direct continuation of Dave: 'Wouldn't it be nice, just once in a blue moon, I should get a proper greeting from my grandson when he sees me?'

Dave . . . grandson when he sees me? Like, 'Hello, Grandpa. How are you, Grandpa? Sorry I haven't seen you in so long, since poor Grandma died. I know you don't get out much these days, Grandpa. But maybe I could come round and give you a hand with a few things, Grandpa!' EH? Danny. Danny!

Danny Yes what is it, Dave?

Dave Is that acceptable behaviour?

Danny Dave – please!

Dave No, no, come on! He walks in, he ignores me, he ignores you, he ignores whatsisname. He's completely *shtum*. He stands there like a spare prick. I mean, is that normal, reasonable, civilised behaviour?

Josh CHANGE THE FUCKING RECORD, WILL YOU?!

Danny Josh, please!

Josh PLEASE! PLEASE! PLEASE! I'M NOT DOING ANYONE ANY HARM! I JUST WANT SOME PEACE. IS THAT TOO MUCH TO ASK?!

Rachel and Tammy rush into the room.
The following segments are simultaneous and shouted. They all start as soon as is feasible after Josh: 'CHANGE THE FUCKING RECORD, WILL YOU?!'

1

Josh CHANGE THE FUCKING RECORD, WILL YOU?!

Dave Oh, the rabbi's come to life! The rabbi's come to life! He's come to life!

He starts an emphysema (coughing) attack, which has passed its climax by the time Danny goes to answer the front door.

2

Josh CHANGE THE FUCKING RECORD, WILL YOU?!

Danny Josh, please!

Rachel and Tammy rush into the room.

Rachel What the hell is going on? I go out of the room for one minute, I come back, and – stop calling him a rabbi! Stop calling him a rabbi!

She rushes over to Dave, who is having his attack, and stands by him.

3

Josh CHANGE THE FUCKING RECORD, WILL YOU?!

Danny Josh, please!

Rachel and Tammy rush into the room.

Tammy Holy shit! Josh – do you mind?! I've got a guest here! I am so sorry about this! I'll go and get him a glass of water.

A few moments later, she returns with the water.

There you go, Grandpa.

4

Josh CHANGE THE FUCKING RECORD, WILL YOU?!

Danny Josh, please!

Rachel and Tammy rush into the room.

No, it's alright. He's winding him up, he's flying off the handle – look, no – you don't have to. (*to Josh*) CALM DOWN!

As Dave is having an attack, and the above cacophony reaches its climax, the front doorbell rings.

Danny Now who's that, for Christ's sake?!

Danny goes out to answer the door while Rachel attends to Dave. Tammy stands in the hall, just outside the room, to see who it is. Tzachi hovers in the doorway.

Josh has retired to the conservatory. The following interchange is not heard clearly, but we can hear a good deal of Michelle's sobbing.

Danny Fucking hell!

Michelle Danny!

After some moments, Rachel realises who it is, and rushes out to the hall. Much sobbing and hugging can be heard. Michelle appears by the door, and kisses Tammy. Then she comes into the room, followed by Rachel and Danny, and then Tammy.
Dave is much absorbed with his attack, and for the moment is oblivious to Michelle, or to anything else.
Michelle stops just inside the room.

Michelle Dad!

He doesn't respond.

Dad!

Rachel He's just had an attack.

Michelle What d'you mean?

Rachel Emphysema.

Michelle (*over-reacting*) Oh!!!

Rachel He's alright – he's alright!

Michelle Is he living here now?

Danny No.

Rachel No, he still lives at home, Mash.

Michelle throws herself into a kneeling position at his feet, sobbing, and buries her face in his trousers. Dave is horrified.

Dave (*eventually*) Get off of me!

Face still down, Michelle strokes Dave's chest.

FUCK OFF!

Rachel Dad!

Michelle collapses back, remaining on the floor. Rachel kneels beside her.

Michelle I don't believe this. Did you hear what he said to me?

Rachel Yes.

Michelle Is that a way for a father to speak to his own daughter?

Rachel He's not well, Mash – you have to make allowances.

Michelle I should make allowances?

Rachel Yes!

Michelle I'm the one that's in mourning!

Rachel We're all in mourning!

Michelle I'm the one that's grieving, I'm the one that's just found out my mother's died!

Rachel You just found out?

Michelle Yes. Why didn't you tell me she was ill?

Rachel She wasn't ill.

Danny (*simultaneously*) She wasn't ill, Mash.

Michelle What d'you mean, she wasn't ill?

Rachel She wasn't ill.

Michelle What, she just suddenly died?

Rachel Yes.

Michelle People don't just suddenly die for no reason.

Rachel She was seventy-six.

Michelle Well, that's not old.

Rachel Maybe not, but she still died.

Danny You hadn't seen her for eleven years.

Michelle Eleven years! That's ridiculous!

Danny No, it's not! None of us have seen you for eleven years – your mum and dad haven't seen you for eleven years –

Michelle (*under Danny*) Eleven years!

Rachel (*under Danny*) Yes!

Danny – eleven years. We haven't seen you for eleven years – the last time we saw you was round about –

Rachel Was shortly after my fortieth birthday, and I'm now fifty-one!

Michelle No, I'm sorry – you're wrong. It wasn't your birthday, it was Danny's birthday. And it wasn't eleven years ago.

Danny No, that's not possible. 'Cos every time my birthday comes round, we're away on holiday.

Rachel It was my birthday!

Michelle No – I remember, we had a barbecue – it was 1998, which, I am here to tell you, was seven years ago.

Danny No, it was eleven years, and it was Rachel's birthday.

Michelle Listen to you – listen to this!

Danny What?!

Michelle I've just found out my mother's died; I'm traumatised, I'm in shock; my father insults me, and now I've got to put up with this ridiculous interrogation!

Rachel What do you mean, you've just found out?

Michelle I've been away, I've been out of the country.

Rachel I told you.

Danny So where have you been?

Michelle I've been in Africa, as it happens.

Danny What, on business?

Michelle No, on holiday. What, is that a sin?

Rachel What, for three months?

Michelle I took myself away. For me.

Rachel What does that mean?

Danny On your own?

Michelle What are you implying?

Danny I'm just asking: were you by yourself, or were you with somebody else?

Michelle It was for my fortieth birthday, actually. I needed to be in my own inner space. I was celebrating.

Danny So, *mazeltov*!

Michelle I have had the most amazing experience. I've been to the Cradle of Civilisation. I've spent an obscene amount of money, now the whole thing's been negated. I might as well not have bothered!

Danny Oh, that's right – your mother died just to spite you!

Michelle I can't even tell anybody at work. The whole thing is so humiliating!

Rachel What, it's humiliating that your mother died?

Michelle No, it's humiliating that nobody told me that my mother had died.

Rachel We tried to tell you!

Danny We left a message on your answerphone.

Michelle Yes, and I got the message three months too late, thank you very much!

Danny What, and you don't check your messages?

Michelle No, not when I've got my mobile – why didn't you call me on my mobile?

Rachel We tried your mobile – the line was dead.

Danny We must have an old number for you, Mash.

Rachel Have you changed it?

Michelle Yes, of course, several times – but I gave you my new number. On my change-of-address card.

Rachel No –

Danny (*simultaneously*) No, you didn't.

Michelle Yes, I texted you –

Danny No, you didn't.

Michelle I texted everyone.

Rachel Well, you didn't text us.

Michelle Every time I change my number I text everybody I know!

Danny Listen: Rachel even tried to call you at work – didn't you?

Rachel The girl said you'd left the company, and she didn't have a number for you!

Michelle (*getting up*) That is the most ridiculous thing I've ever heard in my life!

Rachel That's what she said!

Michelle That is bollocks – she couldn't have said that!

Rachel No, I made the whole thing up. Where are you going now?

Michelle is standing near the door with her bag over her shoulder.

Michelle I'm not going anywhere.

Tammy Hello! How are you? Good to see you! The last time I saw you, I was marginally shorter. I was younger. But then you were younger yourself. We had a row, but that's water under the bridge now. So meet my friend Tzachi. Tzachi, this is my Auntie Michelle, also known as Mash. Mash, this is Tzachi.

Michelle It's very nice to meet you. (*She shakes his hand.*) What are you, Greek or Turkish?

Tzachi chortles.

Tammy He's an Israeli. From Israel.

Michelle Oh! (*Pause.*) *Shalom.*

Tammy Great! Now that we've dealt with the niceties, would anyone like a cup of tea?

Danny I'd kill for one.

Rachel Thank you, Tammy!

Michelle Yes, please. But I never drink tea. I'll have a coffee instead.

Tammy goes out to the kitchen with Tzachi. Michelle turns to looks at Josh, who is near her, in the conservatory. After a moment, he moves away from her, into the garden. She looks helplessly at Rachel.

Rachel For goodness sake, Mash, come and sit down!

Danny Yes, come on.

Michelle sits on the sofa, and instantly jumps up and darts across the room.

Michelle I can't sit down – I've got *shpilchas in tuchus.*

Danny Mash! Would you please sit down, you're making me nervous.

Dave Sit down, for Christ's sake!

Michelle Alright, Dad!

Rachel Take your jacket off – I'll hang it up for you.

Michelle takes off her jacket and shoves it at Rachel, as if unconsciously behaving rudely to a servant.

Michelle Thank you! (*She sits on the sofa.*)

Rachel You're welcome.

Pause. For a few moments, Michelle takes deep, focusing breaths, evoking myriad alternative therapies and other spiritually purifying practices. Rachel returns.

You alright now, Dad?

Dave Yeah, I'm alright.

Rachel sits. Pause.

Michelle This isn't easy for me.

Danny What, you think it's easy for any of us?

Michelle Well, you've had three months to get over it.

Rachel Get over what?

Michelle Mum.

Rachel Oh, this is something you get over?

Michelle You've had a three-month head start.

Rachel It's not a competition, Mash.

Michelle I can't even picture her face.

Danny Are you surprised?

Michelle Please . . . have a little respect for my feelings.

Rachel Have you stopped to consider our feelings?

Michelle Let me tell you something. In every other area of my life, I'm treated with respect. I've made something of myself – I'm proud of who I've become. I've got a beautiful mews house with no mortgage; I've got a top-of-the-range sports car; I've reached the height of my profession, and that is very hard for a woman, let me tell you. I'm dealing with billions of dollars every day. I am emotionally stable, and very mature. My friends adore me, and tell me I have a hysterical sense of humour. It's only my family that treat me with derision.

Pause.

Rachel You obviously have a wonderful life, Mash.

Michelle Well, yes, I do, thank you very much.

Danny You used to have a great sense of humour, Mash. Remember?

Pause.

Dave Are you married?

Michelle And what sort of question's that?

Dave It's a simple question, in English. Are you married?

Michelle Well, don't you think you'd know about it if I'd got married?

Dave How would I know? Mm? So . . . you're not married; you haven't got a family; but you handle millions of dollars every day; so you're *ungershtokt* with *gelt*, you're stinking rich, and you go on safaris in Africa. But there's one thing I do know.

Michelle And what's that, then?

Dave You're not happy – you're miserable. And I'll tell you something else. You . . . are *mishigah* – you're mad. You need help.

Rachel Dad!

Michelle You know who he sounds like, don't you? He sounds like Mum. That's the way she used to talk to me.

Rachel What are you talking about?

Michelle Nobody will ever know the way that woman treated me.

Dave Why, what did she ever do to you?

Michelle (*getting up*) What are you, blind?

Dave Meaning?

Michelle I'm surprised at you, Dad. I would have thought you'd be relieved, now she's gone.

Rachel How can you say such a thing?!

Danny (*simultaneously*) Oh, Mash, that's disgusting!

Michelle Well, he's the one that always said she was a difficult woman!

Dave A difficult woman, yes! But she was a good wife, and a bloody good mother!

Michelle A bloody good mother! She never treated me like a daughter – she never loved me!

Dave Oh, don't talk so stupid! She loved you exactly the same as she loved your sister!

Michelle Oh? The Golden Girl?

Rachel The Golden Girl? Where's that come from, all of a sudden?

Michelle You could do no wrong, in her eyes. She had you on a pedestal.

Rachel I don't know what you're talking about. I've never heard of any of this before!

Michelle The lovely husband, the son-in-law who's a dentist, the two wonderful grandchildren, the house in Cricklewood. 'She stuck to her principles!'

Danny (*getting up*) You know what, Mash? You turn up here, after God knows how many years, without warning, and you start throwing your weight around, insulting people, and behaving as if you're the only person on the planet who's ever suffered a loss!

Michelle Rachel, let me tell you something. She never wanted me.

Danny Oh, please!

Rachel What?

Michelle She told me.

Rachel She told you that?

Michelle She resented me from the moment I was born.

Rachel Oh, Mash!

Dave I'm telling you, you're dealing with a nutcase.

Michelle See?

Danny I don't believe that, Mash.

Michelle What?

Danny Your mother would never have said that.

Michelle Are you calling me a liar?

Danny Yes, I am calling you a liar!

Michelle (*shouting*) And how would you know? Were you there when we were growing up?

Danny (*shouting*) Yes, I was, a lot of the time, if you recall!

   Rachel get up and joins them.

Rachel (*shouting*) Yes, but you weren't there all the time, Danny, and she and Mum never got on – you know that!

Danny Yes, but there's a big difference, Rachel, between not getting on, and wishing your child had never been born!

Rachel But you're calling my sister a liar!

Danny She is a liar.

Rachel She's my sister!

Danny She is a disingenuous, self-absorbed liar!

Michelle Yes, and she's here, thank you very much, and this is the welcome she gets!

   She throws herself on the sofa. At the same moment, Tammy enters, holding the cake on a plate. Tzachi is behind her with the laden tea tray.

Tammy Fruit cake?

Danny (*indicating Michelle*) Yes – there! I'm sorry.

He goes upstairs.
Rachel joins Tammy and Tzachi at the table, where they are pouring the tea and cutting cake.
Dave is laughing quietly. He is hugely amused.

Dave (*to himself*) Oy a broch!

Rachel (*unamused*) D'you want a cup of tea, Dad?

Dave Yeah, give me a cup.

Rachel goes to the table. Tammy gives Michelle her coffee.

Tammy Coffee, madam?

Michelle (*without irony*) Thank you so much.

Tammy *Mon plaisir.*

Rachel (*cup of tea*) Here you are, Dad.

Michelle This is white coffee.

Tammy And –?

Michelle I don't take milk.

Rachel Why didn't you tell Tammy that when you asked her for coffee?

Tammy Don't worry about it, Mum.

Michelle Most people say, 'Would you like milk and sugar?'

Rachel In restaurants, maybe.

Tammy Would you like milk and sugar?

Michelle No, I wouldn't like milk, thank you very much – my bowel can't tolerate it.

Tammy Maybe that's why you've got issues with your mother.

She takes the coffee out to the kitchen.

Pause. Rachel and Tzachi are at the table. Josh is in the conservatory. During the following, Tzachi goes to Josh. We don't really hear:

Tzachi You want some tea?

Josh Cheers.

They both come into the room and sit by the sideboard.

Michelle I don't want to cause a fuss.

Dave takes out a cigarette.

Why are you still smoking, Dad?

Dave What's it got to do with you?

Michelle I'm your daughter. I care.

Dave Like hell you care.

Michelle Why are you letting him smoke?

Rachel He smokes.

Michelle But he's not well. He should have someone looking after him.

Rachel I'm sorry. Would you care to repeat that remark?

Michelle He's living on his own. He can't cope. Look at him.

Danny enters at some point during the following speech.

Rachel Mash . . . I look after him. I go round there every other day, and when I don't go, I phone. And while you're reducing your *fancy-shmancy* friends to hysterics, and finding your inner peace in the Cradle of Civilisation, d'you know what I'm doing? I'm cooking, and cleaning, and washing, and shopping, and driving, and caring for our father!

Michelle Well, you've got the time on your hands – what else have you got in your life?

Danny How dare you!

Rachel No, it's fine. It's fine. She's absolutely right. I've done nothing with my life. I went to university; I did nothing with my degree. I've never achieved anything; I've never earned a single penny. All I've got to show for the last thirty years is the three people I love, and who love me.

Josh goes out to the garden. During the above, Tammy has entered with the coffee. She stops to listen to Rachel. When Rachel has finished, she gives Michelle the cup, and goes and kisses Rachel on the cheek. Then she joins Tzachi. They whisper during the following.

Rachel, who, throughout the above speech has been holding a piece of cake on a plate, sits by Michelle and strokes her hand.

(*quietly*) I'm sorry, Mash. D'you want a bit of cake?

Michelle (*quietly*) No, I can't eat. I'm all in knots.

Tammy and Tzachi move towards the door, holding hands.

Tammy Mum, I'm just going to take Tzachi on a tour of the rest of the chateau.

Tammy and Tzachi go upstairs.

Michelle He's a nice boy.

Rachel He's a lovely boy. And we only met him for the first time today.

Michelle And you're letting them go upstairs?

Danny What, are you jealous?

Michelle No, of course I'm not jealous – I'm pleased for her!

Pause. Michelle sips the coffee. Then she grimaces.

What is this? Instant? Haven't you got a *cafetière*? I can't drink this!

Rachel Okay, Mash.

Rachel takes Michelle's cup, and puts it on the tray on the table. Then she sits on the arm of the sofa.

Dave What d'you want, the family silver?

Michelle All I want is a drink I can drink. Actually, I'd like a drink drink.

Dave Next time, send us a telegram from the jungle, we'll get a crate of champagne in for you!

Michelle Please, Dad! I don't want a row!

Dave You could have fooled me!

Pause.

Michelle This is nice. Now that we're all sitting calmly, can't we have a proper conversation, like a normal family?

Dave About what, the Revolution?

Michelle About Mum.

Dave What about Mum?

Michelle I need to know what happened.

Dave I'll tell you what happened. She died.

Michelle I know she died.

Dave And while she was alive, not a day passed when she didn't grieve over her youngest daughter. That's what happened.

Michelle Grieve for me? She couldn't care less about me! She knew where I was, she knew where I worked, she knew where I lived, she had all my numbers – why didn't she call me? She never once picked up the phone to me.

Danny So why didn't you phone her?

Michelle I sent her a birthday card. I sent them both a birthday card, every year.

Dave Birthday cards? That's an insult!

Michelle Well, it's more than you sent me!

Danny I'm asking you, Mash: why didn't *you* phone *her*?

Michelle Because I couldn't.

Danny Why not?

Michelle Because nothing I could ever do was good enough. Have a conversation? What would we talk about? We didn't have a relationship.

Danny You never phoned any of us.

Michelle No, because of her – that's what she did to me. And now she's gone, and I miss her terribly – I haven't slept for weeks.

Rachel But you've only just found out.

Pause.

Michelle Well, it feels like weeks.

Pause.

Danny (*quietly*) Mash! Mash, Mash . . .

Michelle I could do with a drink.

Rachel and Danny look at each other. Pause.

What are you saying, I never called you? (*She gets up.*)

I called you just before Tammy went to university –
I called you at the surgery.

Danny Did you?

Michelle Yes, you know I did.

Danny So what d'you want, a medal? Once in eleven years?

Michelle It's not eleven years, it's seven years. It was 1998.

Danny Tammy went to university in 1997, actually, but who's counting?

Michelle (*shouting*) Well, that's not eleven years!

Danny (*shouting*) It's eleven years since you've seen any of us!

Michelle (*shouting*) That's not true!

Danny (*shouting*) Yes, it is!

Michelle (*shouting*) No, it's not!

Tammy and Tzachi have come downstairs. They are in the doorway. Rachel sits down.

Rachel (*quietly*) I sent you a card for your thirtieth birthday. I wrote you a letter. I sent you flowers when you moved. You never responded to any of them. Was that Mum's fault as well?

During the following, Josh comes into the conservatory from the garden.

Michelle Listen to me, Rachel. You know how much I care for these children. I love them desperately. I'm their favourite auntie. They're a major part of my life. Remember how it used to be – all of us here, together? We were happy. I never used to spend any time at home,

102

did I, Dad? I was either here, or at the Movement. I used to come straight round with my blue shirt still on. Remember I used to baby-sit? I used to sleep on the old sofa when this wall was here. Me and Tammy upstairs, having midnight feasts. Remember the pickled herring and the Smarties?

Tammy (*drily*) Yeah, yeah – it was great.

Michelle And me and Josh? I used to take him up to Hampstead Heath with his binoculars. I used to look after them to give you two quality time alone! They used to love me!

Josh bursts from the conservatory.

Josh (*shouting*) That's enough!

Danny Josh, please!

Josh You gave up on us! You let us all down! And now you can't even find it in your heart to say, 'I'm sorry.'

Michelle Josh! Joshie!

She goes towards him with her arms outstretched.

Josh Get the fuck away from me!

He hurtles away from her, to the other end of the room, by the bookcase.

You're disgusting!

Danny Josh!

Dave He's got a point.

Pause.

Michelle Oh, I see. So now the poison's spread to Josh; to my little Joshie. So now you're all against me – my whole family. My father rejects me at the very moment I needed him most. I wanted us to grieve together, Dad, like father and daughter, but what happens? You spit in my face! I don't deserve to be treated like this! My own mother, God rest her soul, what does she do? She dies on my fortieth birthday – typical! My sister sits there, wallowing in her own martyrdom; my brother-in-law hasn't stopped attacking me since the moment I walked through the door –

Danny Mash!

Michelle goes to Tammy.

Michelle And Tammy! What's happened to you? You've become so cynical! You used to be like me – open. None of you appreciate me. I'm not a bad person – I'm a good person. I'm a people person. I'm easy-going – I'm not demanding. Okay, if I've got a fault, it's that I'm too generous – I'm always there for my friends, I never have any time for myself! Why are you doing this to me? All I wanted was to be with my family!

Josh You think you're the only one who suffers, don't you? Well, you're not. We all suffer – life's about suffering! You think you're the victim in this family. Well, you walked away. I'm still stuck with it! My grandpa thinks I'm a waste of space. My parents see me as a religious freak!

Danny Josh!

Josh My sister doesn't understand me at all! And let me tell you something. It's lonely! It's fucking lonely!

He rushes upstairs. Rachel gets up and follows him.

Rachel Josh!

Pause.

Tammy Crikey!

Michelle What's he mean, religious freak? Where's he found religion from, all of a sudden?

Dave Who cares? At least he's found something. What have you found?

Michelle But we never ever used to fast on Yom Kippur in this family.

Dave So what? He's found something that has some meaning for him – something positive. You may not agree with it. I may not agree with it. Actually, I think it's a load of crap – all religion's bollocks. But it means something to him.

Michelle I don't have a problem with it. You couldn't find a more spiritual person than me.

Tammy Amen!

Michelle Listen. If it makes him happy, I'm happy.

Dave Spiritual? Up your *tuchus*, spiritual! You're not spiritual!

Danny Dave!

Rachel returns.

Dave No, no, no – what you do is evil. You're an agent of capitalism! You're a merchant banker! You do your millions of dollars every day, and you don't give a fuck how many people suffer in the process!

Danny Enough, now!

Michelle You're the hypocrite! You're the capitalist! You're the one who always employed people, and made a profit!

Danny Mash!

Michelle I'm not the one who sold out! You were the kibbutznik with the socialist ideals, and what happened? You walked away! You came home, and you set up your pathetic little removals business!

*All hell now breaks loose. Everybody except Tammy
starts screaming and shouting simultaneously. As
follows:*

1

*Beginning after Michelle: '. . . your pathetic little removals
business!' Dave and Michelle talk across each other,
overlapping.*

Dave Pathetic little removals business!

Michelle Yes, it is pathetic!

Dave That business put a roof over your fucking head!

Michelle 'Cos you've never done anything for your own
daughter!

Dave You cunt!

Michelle You're the cunt! I've made something of my
life! I've made money! You're a loser! You've never made
anything of your life! Mum never did anything with her
life, either!

Dave You're a fucking bitch, an ungrateful bitch!

Dave is overcome by an angina attack.

2

*Beginning after Michelle: '. . . your pathetic little removals
business!'*

Rachel That's enough, Mash! You said you came here to
grieve with your family! If you carry on like this, there'll
be another family bereavement – we'll have another
corpse to grieve for!

3

*Beginning after Michelle: '. . . your pathetic little removals
business!'*

Danny I don't know how you've got the gall to look your own father in the face and call him a hypocrite, when you're the biggest hypocrite of them all!

Michelle Me a hypocrite? You're the hypocrite!

Danny I'm not a hypocrite! What have I done to deserve being called a hypocrite?!

4

And somewhere during all of this, Tzachi who has been quietly and patiently watching and listening, suddenly wades into the fray, Israeli commando-style – loudly, boldly, with total authority, and with his hands in the air:

Tzachi Allo! Allo! Allo! Allo! Allo! Allo! Allo! Allo! Allo!

They all shut up.

Enough! It's not funny any more!

Quietly, to Dave, who is having his attack.

Okay?

Danny No, he needs to sit down.

Tzachi helps Danny and Rachel to sit Dave down.

Danny Have you got his pills?

Rachel Here they are. Take the water, Dad.

Michelle has remained standing just where she was when Tzachi's intervention shocked her into silence. Tzachi now turns to her.

Tzachi (*shouting*) Sit!

Michelle doesn't move. Tzachi goes right up to her, and stands face to face with her at very close quarters.

(*shouting*) SIT DOWN!

Pause. Then Michelle sits on the sofa, stunned into what will be a very long silence.

Throughout all of this, Tammy has been observing quietly. When Tzachi intervenes, she says 'Tzachi!' a couple of times, but that is all she says. Her reaction to his intervention is one of loving amusement – she's proud of him, and finds it very funny.

Now, Tzachi joins her, and they hold hands. An immediate sense of sharing the joke.

Dave's attack has now subsided, and Josh has come back and is standing at the conservatory door, looking out at the garden. He is no longer wearing his skull-cap, but nobody has yet noticed this.

Tzachi turns to Rachel and Danny.

Tzachi Er . . . I am very sorry. This is not my business . . . not my family, but . . . I don't want to be here.

Rachel No. Of course not.

Danny I don't blame you, Tzachi. I'd get out while you can, if I were you. (*He shakes Tzachi's hand.*) Er, it's very nice to meet you. You'll bring him round again, won't you, darling? Maybe for a meal, next time?

Tzachi I'd like this.

Rachel It would be nice.

Tzachi Thank you. Goodbye.

Rachel Goodbye.

Tzachi kisses her.

Thank you.

Tzachi goes to Dave, who is sitting in the armchair.

Tzachi Goodbye!

Dave *Le'hitraot.*

Tzachi *Shalom.*

Dave *Shalom.*

They shake hands.

Tzachi Goodbye, Josh!

Josh turns round.

Josh (*quietly*) See you.

Pause.

Tammy Cool. 'Bye, everyone – thanks. It's been . . . fun. We're going to the cinema. 'Bye, Grandpa.

Dave 'Bye, darling.

They kiss.

Tammy Take care. Keep out of mischief. 'Bye, Mum.

Rachel 'Bye, darling.

They kiss.

Tammy Speak to you in the week.

Rachel What are you going to see?

Tammy *Crash.* 'Bye, Dad. (*She kisses Danny.*)

Danny 'Bye, darling.

Tammy picks up her bag.

Tammy You forgot to tell me to take my keys.

Danny Take your keys.

Tammy Thanks, Mash! Good to see you. Great to hear all about you . . . Yeah, it's a shame you didn't get to hear about what I've been up to, but, er . . . well, that would have involved asking questions – which I appreciate you find quite difficult. Yeah, it would've been nice to chew the fat about the big, bad world. But, hey! (*Pause.*) Here's a thought . . . you know, the great thing about being an adult is, you get to take responsibility for yourself. I'm enjoying it immensely. I hope you do too. One day. So . . . *Hasta luego! Viva la Revolución!*

She looks at Josh.

'Bye, Josh.

Josh has his back to the room. He doesn't turn round.

Josh Goodbye, Tammy.

Tammy Are you alright?

Rachel and Danny turn to look at Josh. So does Tzachi. Josh is crying. Neither Dave nor Michelle is aware of this.

(*to Josh*) Take care.

She and Tzachi look at each other. Then they leave.
Rachel goes to Josh, and puts her arm round him.
The front door closes behind Tammy and Tzachi.
Danny moves nearer to Rachel and Josh. He is clearly upset. Dave and Michelle remain oblivious to what is happening to Josh and his parents.
Pause.
The doorbell rings. Michelle retreats further into the sofa.

Danny I don't believe it – she's forgotten her keys!

He goes to answer the door.

Dave (*to Michelle*) If you want a *shluff*, why don't you go upstairs, lay down properly? Oi!

Michelle doesn't respond.
Danny opens the door. The following is hardly audible.

Jonathan (*off*) Hi, Danny.

Danny (*off*) Oh – Jonathan. Erm – sorry, it's not a very good time. Come in, come in . . .

Jonathan (*off*) How are you?

Danny (*off*) Mash is here. I'm just warning you. Go in, go in!

Rachel has moved away from Josh. Enter Jonathan, carrying another box of produce, followed by Danny.

Er, it's the market gardener.

Jonathan Hello, Rachel.

Rachel Hello, Jonathan. What have you brought for us today?

Jonathan A cabbage, some potatoes and a few onions. Enjoy.

Rachel takes the box.

Rachel Thank you.

Danny I'll tell you what.

Jonathan What?

Danny Your courgettes are better than mine.

Jonathan Thanks. Josh! How's it going, mate?

Josh (*quietly*) Hi.

Rachel Would you like a cup of tea, Jonathan?

Jonathan No, I won't stay. Sally's waiting for me.

Rachel takes the box out to the kitchen.

Dave!

He goes to Dave and shakes his hand.

Jonathan Piltz, remember?

Michelle looks round at him.

Dave Who?

Jonathan From way back?

Pause. Dave looks blank.

I heard your sad news. I wish you long life.

Dave Thank you very much.

Jonathan Hello, Mash. Long time no see. How are you?

Michelle looks at him. She seems confused.

It's Jonathan.

Michelle What are you doing here?

Jonathan I just popped in.

Michelle What for?

Jonathan With some vegetables.

Danny He's got an allotment, Mash.

Jonathan It's just round the corner – I was on my way home. So how are you?

Michelle I'm fine, thank you very much – why? Don't I look it?

Jonathan You look great!

Michelle Do I?

Jonathan Yeah.

Rachel returns.

It's been a long time.

Michelle Yeah. Must be ten years.

Rachel No, Mash.

Jonathan More like twenty.

Michelle It's not twenty years.

Danny It is, Mash.

Jonathan Actually, it's twenty-one. 1984. I know – I can't believe it, either.

Rachel No? It seems like a long time ago to me.

Danny It just goes, doesn't it?

Dave Ten years? Twenty years? Fifty years! What's the difference? You still end up in a bloody box!

Rachel Thanks, Dad.

Jonathan So, what you been up to?

Michelle I've been having a tough time, actually. My mother's just passed away.

Dave She's heartbroken.

Jonathan Yeah, I heard. I'm sorry, Mash. I wish you long life.

He sits next to her on the sofa. She touches him.

Michelle Thanks. So . . . what about you? You still married to your little social worker?

Jonathan Yeah, we're very happy – thanks. Are you . . . with anyone?

Michelle No. Yeah – well, not at the moment, exactly, but . . . yeah. So . . . you must have a couple of kids by now?

Jonathan extracts himself from her hold.

Jonathan No. But we're expecting our first in January – (*to Rachel and Danny*) I was going to tell you!

Michelle recoils in anguish.

Rachel Oh, Jonathan, that is wonderful news!

Danny (*overlapping*) Jonathan – that's fantastic!

Rachel kisses Jonathan. Danny shakes his hand.

Jonathan Thank you.

Rachel I'm so thrilled for you both!

Danny (*overlapping*) That's the best news – *mazeltov*!

Jonathan Thank you very much.

Rachel You must send Sally our congratulations!

Jonathan I will.

At some point Josh has come in from the conservatory, and has sat on the small sofa.
Rachel and Danny are very much aware of this.

Josh Congratulations.

Jonathan Thank you.

Dave *Mazeltov!*

Jonathan Thank you very much.

Michelle suddenly jumps up with her bag, and rushes straight out of the room, turning to rush straight back in, to the doorway.

Michelle Excuse me. I'm just going to the toilet. I know: when I get back, why don't we have a drink? To celebrate!

She rushes upstairs.

Rachel She's not having a drink.

Danny Well, what are we going to do? Lock up the booze?

Rachel We don't need to lock it up – we just tell her no.

Danny You try telling her no.

Rachel Danny, it's our house – she can't have a drink without our permission.

Jonathan (*getting up*) Listen, I should be going – Sally's waiting for me. We've got some friends coming round.

Rachel Oh, that's nice!

Jonathan goes to Dave.

Jonathan Dave!

Dave All the best!

They shake hands.

Jonathan Take it easy, Josh.

Josh Goodbye, Jonathan.

Jonathan Nice to see you, Danny.

Jonathan goes out with Rachel and Danny.

Rachel I'm so pleased about your news, Jonathan.

Jonathan Tell me about it!

Danny I had a joke for Sally . . .

Jonathan, Rachel and Danny can hardly be heard in the hall.
Pause.

Josh So, how're you doing, Grandpa?

Dave How d'you think I'm doing?

Josh I'm just asking how you are.

Dave I'm alright, Josh. I'm surviving. (*He gets up.*) How about you? How are you doing?

The front door closes.

Josh I'll get by.

Dave Good!

Rachel and Danny return.

Listen, Rachel. I don't think I could stand another one of your sister's *mishiginah* party pieces. Danny can take me home, preferably not via Manchester.

Danny You're right, but if you don't want to see her, we'd better go now.

Dave *Kim schoen*. Thank you.

Dave exits, followed by Rachel and Danny.

Rachel (*going*) I'll phone you tomorrow, Dad.

Dave (*going*) Yes. Listen – Monday, can you take that watch to the mender's for me? I can't see through the glass. You promised.

Rachel (*off*) I promised, and I'll do it.

Danny (*off*) Get a move on.

Dave (*off*) Well, open the door . . .

Pause. Then Josh gets up and disappears into the garden. The front door closes. Rachel comes back into the empty room. She glances into the garden, and starts to collect up the tea things.
    Michelle comes downstairs and enters the room. She stops in her tracks. She looks around.

Michelle Where's everybody gone?

Rachel They've gone.

She loads up the tea tray.

Michelle I only went upstairs to do a wee. What did I say? What did I do? What did you tell them? I thought we were going to have a party. Why didn't they wait to say goodbye? Rachel, why are you doing this to me? Rachel!

Rachel has picked up the tea tray. She stops in the doorway and looks at Michelle. Then she goes out to the kitchen.
   Pause.

I don't fucking need this!

She rushes out of the room. Josh appears in the conservatory. He looks into the room. Michelle comes back, pulling on her jacket. Josh ducks out of her view. She heads straight for the sideboard, grabs a bottle of whisky, opens it, takes a couple of swigs, puts the bottle back, throws the bottle cap on the floor, and runs out.

(*shouting, off*) THANK YOU!

The front door slams. Josh picks up the bottle cap, and looks at it. Pause. Fade to blackout.

SCENE TWO

Lights up. A few days later. Night. The curtains are drawn and the lights are on.
   Rachel is reading the Guardian *in the armchair. Danny and Josh are playing chess at the table.*
   Pause.

Rachel If I believed in fate, I'd say it was some kind of judgement on them. How could they have got it so badly wrong? That's what I'd like to know. How could they not have seen it coming?

Danny Well, we all knew it was coming, didn't we?

Josh Yeah, we saw it on the telly.

Danny Heading straight for New Orleans.

Rachel So how come they didn't have an evacuation plan?

Danny Because they expected everybody to get out under their own steam. In their cars.

Rachel What, they expected people like this to get out under their own steam?

She shows them the newspaper.

Look at these women.

Danny and Josh come and join her to take a closer look at the photograph.

And the worst of it is, about a third of the Louisiana National Guard is in Iraq. With equipment that could've helped with the rescue effort.

Danny What, you think they're gonna learn from this?

Rachel That'll be the day.

Danny So . . .

Josh Makes you realise how vulnerable you are. One minute you exist. Next minute, gone.

Rachel Yeah. And you always think it's going to happen to someone else.

Danny So God says to Noah . . . 'Next time there's a flood, I don't want any animals in the ark. Only fish. But not any old fish. Just carp. In big glass tanks.' And he says, 'Noah: think big. I want eight levels, at least.' So Noah goes, 'Ah! I get you, God. What you're asking me to build is a multi-storey Carp Ark!'

They all laugh.

Rachel Not bad.

Josh Come on, Dad.

Josh and Danny return to their game of chess.

Danny Whose go is it?

Josh It's yours.

Pause. Danny makes a move. They both ponder the board. Rachel reads the newspaper. Slow fade to blackout.

Glossary

It isn't possible to give full notes on pronunciation, other than to say that in the Yiddish and Hebrew words, 'ch' is as in 'loch', not 'ch' as in 'child'.

Aliyah (Hebrew) 'To go on Aliyah' is to emigrate to Israel from the diaspora.

B'seder (Hebrew) In order, okay.

Bar mitzvah (Hebrew) When a Jewish boy reaches manhood at thirteen.

Baruch Atah etc. (Hebrew) Blessed are You, the Lord our God, King of the Universe, who has sanctified us with His Commandments, and commanded us to put on *tefillin*.

Cafetière (French) A sophisticated style of coffee percolator.

Capple (Yiddish) Skull-cap

Chalutz (Hebrew) Pioneer.

Chassidim (Hebrew) Fundamentalist orthodox Jews. The Chassidic movement began in Poland in the eighteenth century. Today its adherents shun modernity, put prayer, ritual and religious celebration above all else, and still dress in an archaic style.

Chaverim (Hebrew) Friends, comrades.

Chochem (Yiddish) A clever-clogs, a smart alec.

Fancy-shmancy (Anglo-Yiddish) Fancy, pretentious, toffee-nosed.

Frummer (Yiddish) A religious or orthodox Jew.

Ganzer (Yiddish) Big, extreme.

Gurnisht (Yiddish) Nothing.

Habonim (Hebrew) 'The Builders'. British secular Socialist Zionist Jewish youth movement, founded in 1929, and linked to several kibbutzim in Israel, including Dave's Kfar Hanassi. This is the movement referred to in the play. Members wore a blue shirt.

Hasta luego (Spanish) See you soon.

Hebrew University The Jewish University at Jerusalem.

Hora (Hebrew) Israeli national circle dance, originating from Eastern Europe.

Kaddish (Hebrew) The Prayer for the Dead.

Kasam (Arabic/Hebrew) A home-made bomb fuelled by fertiliser, alcohol, etc.

Kibbutz (Hebrew) Jewish collective settlement in Israel.

Kibbutzniks (Hebrew) Members of a kibbutz.

Kim schoen (Yiddish) Come quickly, let's get on with it.

Kippah (Hebrew) Skull-cap.

Kvetching (Yiddish) Grumbling, whingeing.

L'chaim (Hebrew) 'To life!' – i.e. 'Cheers!'

Le'hitraot (Hebrew) See you again.

Luboviches (properly *Lubaviches*) A particular Chassidic sect founded in Lubavici, Russia, in the eighteenth century. A proselytising movement, now controlled from New York.

Ma ha-shaah? (Hebrew) What time is it?

Ma shlomchah? (Hebrew) How are you?

Madre mia (Spanish) Holy Mother!

Mazeltov (Hebrew) Congratulations.

Mechullah (Yiddish) Bankrupt.

Meshugah (Yiddish/Hebrew) Mad.

Mikvah (Hebrew) Jewish ritual bath-house. Mostly used by women.

Mishigah, mishiginah (Yiddish) Mad.

Mishigas (Yiddish) Madness.

Momzers (Yiddish) Bastards.

Mon plaisir (French) My pleasure.

Motzah balls (Hebrew) Dumplings, made from egg and *matzah* meal. Usually eaten in chicken soup, never for breakfast. *Matzah* is the biscuit-like unleavened bread eaten at Passover. Dave says '*motzah*', the East End pronunciation.

No, tu eres grandpa (Spanish) No, you are a grandpa.

Noch (Yiddish) To boot, yet, even, already.

Nu? (Yiddish) Well?

Och a nebbish! (Yiddish) Ah, what a sad loser!

Oy a broch! (Yiddish) What a mess!

Plotzing (Yiddish) Sweating, getting het up.

Potz (Yiddish) Vagina (used pejoratively).

Rebbe (Yiddish) Rabbi ('What, a rabbi with a long white beard?')

Reva le'arbah (Hebrew) Quarter to four.

Rikudim (Hebrew) Israeli dances.

Ruach (Hebrew) Spirit, collective energy.

Shalom (Hebrew) Peace! (Israeli greeting.)

Sheitl (Yiddish) Wig worn by an orthodox Jewish married woman, whose hair mustn't be seen by any man other than her husband.

Shiksa (Yiddish/Hebrew) A non-Jewish girl.

Shlepping (Yiddish) Carrying, doing heavy work.

Shluff (Yiddish) A sleep.

Shluffing (Yiddish) Sleeping.

Shmackel (Yiddish) Penis.

Shmock (Yiddish) Idiot (literally, penis).

Shpilchas in tuchus (Yiddish) Pins, sparklers or firecrackers up the arse, on tenterhooks, ants in the pants.

Shtum (Yiddish) Silent.

Shul (Yiddish) Synagogue.

Si, es muy complicado (Spanish) Yes, it's very complicated.

Slicha (Hebrew) Sorry.

Sub judice (Latin) Under judicial consideration. Banned from discussion.

Tchutchela (Yiddish) Little angel.

Tefillin (Hebrew/Aramaic) Two black leather boxes containing Biblical passages, each attached to a leather strap. These are bound round the left arm, and attached to the forehead, respectively. Orthodox Jewish men put them on and pray at dawn every weekday. In English, they are called phylacteries.

Torah (Hebrew) The Old Testament, the Laws of Moses, the whole concept of Judaism.

Tov, todah (Hebrew) Good, thank you.

Tuchus (Yiddish) Bottom, arse.

Ungershtokt with gelt (Yiddish) Stuffed with money.

Viva la Revolución! (Spanish) Long live the Revolution!

Yiddles (Yiddish) Jews.

Yofi. Ma nishmah? (Hebrew) Lovely. What's with you?

Yom Kippur (Hebrew) The Day of Atonement, when observant Jews fast in repentance for their sins.